From Topic to Defense: Writing a Quality Social Science Dissertation in 18 Months or Less

*An active reference guiding you
from concept through completion*

Ayn Embar-Seddon O'Reilly
Michael K. Golebiewski
Ellen Peterson Mink

ISBN: 1499604130
ISBN-13: 978-1499604139

CONTENTS

ABOUT THE AUTHORS

Ayn Embar-Seddon O'Reilly

Ayn earned her undergraduate degrees in philosophy and psychology from the University of Pittsburgh. She holds a master's degree in clinical psychology from Edinboro University of Pennsylvania. She earned her Ph.D. in criminology from Indiana University of Pennsylvania after completing a qualitative case study on hospital violence for her dissertation.

She began working with doctoral level students in 2001. It was through years of helping many, many students work on their dissertations that this helpful little book was born. She has previously published a forensic science textbook, and co-authored *Completing Your Qualitative Study*.

Michael K. Golebiewski

Michael has a certification in Marketing and earned his master's degree in Multimedia Technology from Duquesne University. He has taught as an adjunct professor in the fields of Multimedia and English Writing at Duquesne University and Carnegie Mellon University, respectively. He has worked for more than 20 years in professional services, honing his project management skill set and keen attention to detail, and has served as an editor on numerous student dissertations. He also co-authored *Completing Your Qualitative Study*.

Ellen Peterson Mink

Ellen earned her undergraduate degree in Psychology from the State University College at Oneonta. She earned her doctorate in Counseling Psychology from the University of Buffalo after completing a quantitative dissertation on infant temperament and toddler behavior in families with alcoholic and non-alcoholic fathers. She worked for 15 years on several large-scale, federally funded, longitudinal grants focusing on child development and family dynamics in families dealing with addiction. She began mentoring doctoral students in 2009. She also co-authored *Completing Your Qualitative Study*.

PREFACE TO THE TEXT

Earning a doctorate degree requires commitment, perseverance, and personal sacrifice—placing some things in our lives on hold. It is, by no means, easy—and there really is nothing that can make it "easy." Any terminal degree that is worth earning is going to be a challenging process—it is important to accept that fact upfront. However, that does not mean that you can't lighten the burden on yourself. Navigating through the coursework can be formidable, but the dissertation—which is unique research—is even more challenging, and there are many stumbling blocks on the way to finishing. Let's face it: doctoral coursework is really not all that different from previous coursework—to have gotten where you are, you already know how to successfully navigate coursework. Unless you are fortunate enough to have previous academic research experience—a previous Ph.D., or prior academic writing experience—you have little in your academic background that really prepares you for the dissertation process. This book is designed to help you surmount the most common stumbling blocks you are likely to encounter on your way to finishing the dissertation. It is not only intended for graduate students who need to finish the dissertation quickly—those who need to get it done, get it done well, and also get it done quickly—but also for all graduate students who believe that everything is in the preparation.

Here are some suggestions for how this book can be used to assist you with completing your dissertation:

1. If you are just beginning your doctoral studies and you bought this book to be prepared for the challenges you will be facing, you may want to read through the entirety of the text—which can reasonably be done in a day or so, and then use the strategies suggested for long-range dissertation planning. You can then revisit the book every so often to make sure you are still on track.

2. You can use the book for planning your time. The book will provide suggestions regarding when you should be working on different portions of the dissertation. Using a timeline can help you move through your proposal and the entire dissertation in a more efficient fashion.

3. You can use this book for structure. So much about the dissertation process can be vague. You are told to write a proposal, but no one really tells you how or when it needs to be done. You can use this book to provide structure, to help explain what you need to do and when.

4. You can use the book as a diagnostic tool to analyze where your weaknesses lie, so that you can put most of your effort into addressing these issues and prevent them from derailing you. It can help you determine if you have strong writing skills, strong research skills and good planning skills.

5. You can use everything in the book—from front to back and back to front—ignoring nothing. The more tools you have, the better you will do.

6. You can use this book to help you if you are already in dissertation and need help making up for lost time.

This text is full of advice and tips that you can use, in whole or in part. Instead of following a traditional chapter layout, it is organized into relevant "mini topics" that are short, easy to read, and backed up by activities and thought exercises which will help determine where you are in the process—and move you forward. Your dissertation is like any other challenge in life: There is no singular "right" way to approach it. It all comes down to finding whatever works for you. We encourage you to read the opening section of this book and then skim the rest to see what it has to offer you. Once you have finished with this brief read-through and realize the potential of its flexibility, you can decide how you will use the book. Remember—you can always use this book in varying ways at different times depending on what your needs are—being mindful that these needs will evolve—that is one of the benefits of the flexibility of this text.

The Project Management Focus of the Book

This book takes a project management approach to the dissertation. Regardless of how daunting the dissertation might seem, it really is a school project—and looking at it as such can help you to focus and get it done. Project management is aimed specifically at being able to complete the task that you have in front of you. The topics that comprise this book are organized into clusters that correspond to the five stages of project management: initiation, planning, execution, monitoring, and closing.

The **initiation** stage focuses on understanding the nature of the project that you are undertaking. During this stage, you will need to familiarize yourself with the dissertation requirements of your university and your department. A failure to really understand what the dissertation is (as with any project) will severely hamper your chances for success.

The **planning** stage consists of allocating your time, and resources (including financial expenses) to the task: completing your dissertation. Risk management is also a part of planning. You will develop a schedule for the dissertation process and you will focus on specific deliverables along the path of completion. You will also need to assess your personal resources to complete the dissertation and, at the same time, address possible deficiencies. You should look at your budget for completing the dissertation—not only in terms of cost of schooling but also expenses related to research, and also the less tangible "cost" of time away from work or from family.

Execution is the processes used to complete the project. This involves writing the dissertation proposal, conducting the research, and the final write-up of the research as the completed dissertation.

Monitoring employs processes that aid in flagging potential pitfalls in the project, while also keeping track of the how the project is progressing. Many people do not actively monitor the progress of their dissertation process nor are they aware of what could potentially go wrong. While monitoring, you will also identify possible corrective actions that need to be taken to keep you—or get you back—on track. You will also pay particular attention to feasibility issues that may arise.

Closing is naturally the conclusion of the project. It involves the activities of final editing of the dissertation, defending the dissertation, and the last administrative steps involved in graduation. While closing, you will also begin to consider what you will do with the dissertation after graduation, because, believe it or not—there is life after graduation!

Topic Cluster: Initiation

The initiation stage focuses on understanding the nature of the project that you are beginning. During this stage, you will need to look into and understand the dissertation requirements of your university and any additional requirements your department. You will need to familiarize yourself with the appropriate style manual for use in formatting your dissertation. A failure to really understand what the dissertation is (as with any project) will severely hamper your chances for success. The following topics are included in the initiation cluster:

- What is the Dissertation?
- The Dissertation Process
- Constructing Your Committee

Topic: What is the Dissertation?

Let's begin by asking ourselves a very simply question: "What is a dissertation?" A dissertation is a book. A dissertation is unique research. A dissertation is a school project. A dissertation is also a process. You may have written a Master's thesis during your schooling; while there *are* similarities between a master's thesis and a dissertation, the dissertation is generally longer, more complex, and must involve *unique* research. You may have previously published academic research articles. Again, there are similarities between academic research articles and a dissertation, but the dissertation often must include theory and a dissertation, at most institutions, cannot simply be a replication study.

Let's also consider what the dissertation is *not*. It is *not* an opinion piece. It is *not* your life's work. It is *not* a way to set out to prove something. It is *not* a way to solve a problem that you've seen in the workplace (unless you are engaged in action research).

A dissertation is not an opinion piece because it is academic research backed up by data. While many academic writing opportunities exist where providing and defending an opinion is encouraged, the dissertation is not one of them. In the dissertation, everything that is known and presented is derived from, research.

A dissertation is not your life's work. You certainly do not want to spend the rest of your life conducting your dissertation research and writing your dissertation. This would keep you at the level of "beginner researcher." You would also be earning less than a Ph.D. would earn. However, it is very common for academics to conduct dissertation research on a topic area that they love and will continue to develop and build upon for their entire careers. It is better to think of the dissertation as your *beginning* research—the place where you really get your feet wet in research. It can be the beginning of doing your life's work.

The dissertation is not the appropriate vehicle to use to set out to "prove something." If you start your research knowing that you will "prove" something, then your entire research study will be biased. Research is not about "proving" something; it is about answering research questions and allowing the data that is collected to speak for itself. Further, you do not need to worry about your dissertation showing statistical significance or finding support for your research hypotheses—that is not the point of a dissertation. Even if you "find nothing" (i.e., the findings are not statistically significant) in your dissertation—your dissertation will still be done. In conducting dissertation research, you should be open to what the data has to say; post-dissertation you can use the results of your study to go on to build other research.

Dissertations—with the exception of action research—are not a way to solve a problem at work. Most workplaces do not take into account "best-practices" and their problems are rarely reflective of the concerns of academic literature. So while the results of research can often be applied in a workplace, most dissertation research leaves workplace problems to those who are conducting "action research." Action research applies to one situation only—the workplace in which it is conducted, but dissertation research must have wider applicability. The aim of dissertation research is to move the academic literature forward.

Perhaps most importantly, do not make more out of the dissertation than it truly is. Don't see the dissertation as an extension of yourself. Many students get sidetracked by trying to change the world with their dissertation; don't aim for a Nobel Prize—aim to complete a well-executed, useful study and get the dissertation done. While there are some individuals who write discipline-altering dissertations, you likely will have a better opportunity to do higher-level work after earning your Ph.D. In fact, many academicians will spend much of their career building upon their dissertation research.

Topic: The Dissertation Process

Writing the dissertation is the culmination of the doctoral process. It is the final hurdle that you must clear before you can graduate with the Ph.D. It moves you from being a passive receiver of knowledge (through coursework) to being an active creator of knowledge (through conducting unique research that will advance your discipline.). The dissertation phase of your doctoral studies begins after you have completed coursework and after you have passed your comprehensive exams. Keep in mind that even though you do not *officially* begin the dissertation process until this point, this does not mean that you cannot begin preparing for the dissertation as early as at the beginning of your doctoral studies. In fact, this entire book is designed to help you do as much groundwork as possible before the official beginning of the dissertation phase of your doctoral program.

This section presents a brief outline of the entire dissertation process from start to finish; each step of the process is discussed in greater detail later in the book. This is designed simply to orient you to the process. Please note that while there are differences among universities and departments regarding the steps in the dissertation process, they are generally as follows:

- Choosing a topic
- Choosing a dissertation chair or mentor
- Choosing your committee
- Writing the proposal
- Defending the proposal
- Conducting your research
- Analyzing your data
- Writing the dissertation
- Defending the dissertation

Choosing a Topic

It's a good idea to begin considering possible dissertation topics early in your doctoral studies, so that you have plenty of time to read and digest the academic literature. Topics come from many places, including areas that have interested you during your coursework, research that you have been involved in at the master's and doctoral level, the "suggestions for future research" sections of recent dissertations, and the latest journals in your discipline. Regardless of where your idea for a topic comes from, most basically it must be connected to your discipline and it must further the academic literature in your discipline.

Choosing a Dissertation Chair or Mentor

The dissertation chair—sometimes referred to as a "dissertation mentor"—is a faculty member who will guide you through the dissertation process. At some institutions you will choose the individual who will be your chair, at other institutions that person will be assigned to you. If you are able to choose your dissertation chair, we suggest that you choose your chair after selecting a topic because you will want a chair who has good knowledge of your topic—and perhaps who may have also conducted research in that area. Some doctoral students specifically apply to their doctoral program because of the research one or more faculty members are conducting. Your chair will also help you choose your other committee members. Because your chair is key to your progress through the dissertation process, make sure that you can establish a good working relationship with this person.

Choosing Your Committee

The committee should be made up of individuals who can help you through your dissertation process. They should have skills to assist you along the way, for example, extensive knowledge of theory, facility with complex statistical procedures, or experience utilizing qualitative approaches. If you are conducting a quantitative study, you will have quantitative faculty members on your committee; likewise, if you are conducting a qualitative study, you will have qualitative faculty members on your committee. As in the selection of your chair, make sure that these individuals can, and are willing to, work with you to help you create the best dissertation possible.

Writing the Proposal

A proposal is a written description of what you want to do for your research. Not all schools utilize a proposal in the dissertation process; some utilize a prospectus, which is more of an outline form of the study that you propose to conduct for your research. For those schools who do utilize a proposal, it is generally comprised of the first three chapters of your dissertation: the Introduction, the literature review, and the methodology. It is written in future tense. The introduction simply lays out the proposal and—like any introduction—presents to the reader what will be contained in the following chapters. The literature review (you've probably written many at this point in your academic career) will review all of the literature that is necessary to provide the backdrop for your study. The methodology (sometimes also called "method") will detail for the reader the step-by-step process of how you plan to carry out your research from how you will choose your subjects to how you will analyze your data.

Defending the Proposal

Many schools will also conduct a formal defense of the proposal. Depending upon the school, this can be a mere "rubber-stamp" of your approved proposal—or it can be a very rigorous defense of your proposed research. During your defense, you will present your proposal to your committee (and possibly others who attend) and you will answer questions about your proposed research. At the conclusion of the defense, a decision will be made by the committee to determine if you will be permitted to proceed into the data collection process of the dissertation.

Collecting Your Data

This is the process of actively going out and conducting your research to obtain your data. This part of the dissertation may last days or months—or even years. If you utilize secondary data, you will not need to conduct research at all, but you must obtain the secondary data set from whomever owns the data set.

Analyzing Your Data

After the data is collected, it must be analyzed. Even if you are utilizing secondary data, instead of collecting your own, you will still need to analyze the data. If you conduct a quantitative study you will perform some sort of statistical analysis on the data. The key here is understanding how to use statistics and how to choose and carry out the appropriate analysis. If you conduct a qualitative study, you will generally be analyzing verbal data through a variety of specialized qualitative techniques.

Writing the Dissertation

The most basic social science dissertation consists of five chapters. If you previously wrote a proposal, you will take your proposal chapters and rewrite them changing them to past tense while including appropriate additional information that covers what has changed since you wrote the proposal. Chapter 1 will now introduce the entire dissertation. Chapter 2 will be expanded to account for any new literature that has been published since you wrote the proposal. Chapter 3 will discuss the methodology—but in past tense—accounting for anything that has changed since the proposal. You will also need to write chapters 4 and 5: the results and discussion chapters. This is a highly reiterative process of writing and revising and honing to produce a smooth finished product.

Defending the Dissertation

Once the dissertation has been written and revised, the last step in the process is to formally defend the dissertation. This will take place in front of your committee. Many schools have the defense open to other individuals who wish to watch. My own dissertation defense was attended by a number of other doctoral students who were preparing for their own defenses. Like the proposal defense, the dissertation defense is usually a process where you briefly present your research and then respond to questions posed to you about the research. In my experience, most dissertation chairs will not allow their students to proceed to the defense unless they are in good shape to pass the defense. However, we have heard of cases where students who received a lot of help writing or conducting statistical analysis for their dissertations, could not answer questions regarding the dissertation to the satisfaction of the committee, and therefore failed the defense.

Topic: Constructing Your Committee

We cannot stress enough how important your choice of a dissertation chair and the composition of your committee is for your work in dissertation—and also for your sanity. Perhaps the most important thing you will do during your time in dissertation is to choose the members of your committee; the most important member of the committee is the dissertation chair.

Choosing Your Chair

The chair is the person who guides the committee and is in charge of your committee. This person will play a variety of roles in your overall dissertation process, so it is important that you choose a good chair. Do some background research prior to choosing a dissertation chair. The dissertations that he or she has chaired are available from UMI dissertation abstracts. Take a look at the dissertations that have been completed. You may also want to consider contacting some of these students to ask about their personal experiences. If they had positive experiences, they should be more than happy to talk to you and make recommendations—even students who have had negative experiences will generally be willing to talk.

The following qualities should be looked for:
1. Working chemistry
2. Accessibility
3. Well-versed in your topic
4. Well-versed in your methodological approach
5. Can provide advice on the total composition of the committee
6. Can help you navigate department politics

Working chemistry. The most important quality to look for in a dissertation chair is that you are able to work well with this person—that the two of you have a good working chemistry. This does not mean that your chair will just sign off on everything you do. It is the job of this person to challenge you to do your best work. On the other hand, you do not want a faculty member who so difficult he or she will stand in your way and present a barrier to the completion of your dissertation. One of the best ways to be able to gauge how well you will work with a faculty member is to audit the interactions you have had with that faculty member in the classroom as an instructor. How were your experiences with this person previously? It is an excellent idea to try to take courses from a variety of the faculty in your department, so that you have a broad pool of candidates to consider as chair and committee. If you cannot do this, talk to other students who have worked with this faculty member and ask what their experience was like.

Accessibility. Your chair must be accessible to you. Since your chair will be guiding you through a very complex process, he or she must be reasonably available to you to answer questions. While this doesn't mean returning emails within the hour, it does mean returning emails within a reasonable amount of time, for example, within the week. This person should also let you know when they will not be available—for example, holidays. Your chair needs to be accessible for everything from entire dissertation reads to the fielding of minor questions. This person should also be able to give you advice in general. While some chairs practically serve as therapists for their students—we wouldn't recommend this. If you need a therapist, go to a qualified therapist and don't burden your chair with issues that are outside of the scope of professional duty.

Well-versed in your topic. If possible, your chair should know your topic area. If he or she has published in that area, so much the better, but experience in closely related topic areas is also good. You might also consider a chair who knows the theory that you will be using for your dissertation very well. The chair should be able to advise you regarding the feasibility of your topic—this would include letting you know if you are trying to research an area that already is over-researched or if the risk-level of your study will not be acceptable to your university's Institutional Review Board. The advantage of having a chair that knows your research area well is that he or she will be able to give you suggestions of where you should look for literature. My own dissertation chair was very helpful to me in the area of theory—since we knew very little about how theory worked within a dissertation at that time.

Well-versed in your methodological approach. The dissertation chair should be adept in the methodological approach you plan to use in your research and analysis. Be wary of dissertation chairs who insist that all of their students adopt a single methodological approach. This could lead to your study being forced into a methodology that is not appropriate for it. On the other hand, your chair should also be able to tell you honestly if your discipline or your department is more welcoming of one methodology over another— or even of one statistic over another. Be mindful that there are many disciplines and many departments that are not welcoming of qualitative research. Be sure that your dissertation will be accepted in both your discipline and your department.

Can provide advice on the total composition of the committee. This individual should also be able to advise you regarding the ideal composition of your committee, and should be able to work with all members of this committee. Universities have different guidelines for the number of members that must sit on a committee; they generally range from three to five members. Some universities allow or encourage individuals outside of the university to sit on committees when appropriate, while others do not. Familiarize yourself with the guidelines for your institution. Your chair should be able to offer suggestions of possible committee members if you ask. It is perfectly acceptable for a chair to tell you which faculty members they feel would work well on your committee and which faculty members might not. Be wary of a chair that bad-mouths other faculty members in response to your query.

Each committee member should be able to work well with your chair and ideally will "bring something to the table." It is always good to have individuals who are well versed in the method you are using. If you are conducting a qualitative study, yet all of the individuals on your committee feel that qualitative is not a worthwhile approach or lack experience with the approach, this will become very problematic during your dissertation. If everyone on your committee knows your topic, that's a plus, and even better if one or more of them knows it very well. While almost all faculty members have some theoretical background, if one or more of your committee members is well versed in the theory you are using, so much the better.

Help you navigate department politics. There is a level of friction in every academic department in every school. It is difficult as a student to be aware of exactly what the working relationships are among the faculty and staff, but you must be very careful not to become involved in departmental politics. The last thing you need is to get caught in the crossfire between two faculty members who have something to prove—especially while in your dissertation process. We have known students who inadvertently put faculty who were enemies on their committees—which led to one faculty member always going against what the other faculty member wanted. In all cases, it made the dissertation process much harder than it had to be. Your chair should never involve you in departmental politics and should help you steer clear of difficulties. However, if your chair says that he or she prefers not to work with someone, you should respect that choice.

Interviewing a Chair. While you probably will not conduct a formal interview for your dissertation chair, you should have conversations with a number of potential chairs. Anyone who is a potential chair should be willing to have a conversation with you—after all, if they can't have a conversation with you now that speaks volumes to how accessible they might be in the future. Below are some suggestions of questions for your potential chair, with space for you to write your own questions. (Many of these are also examples of how a qualitative interview question might be written for a research study.)

Chair Interview Questionnaire.

1. What excites you about chairing dissertations?
2. What do you see as the goal of the dissertation?
3. Are there certain topics that you particularly enjoy guiding through dissertation?
4. Do you favor a particular method? If so, why?
5. How do you prefer to communicate with your dissertation students?
6. How many dissertations have you chaired?
7. How many dissertations are you chairing now?
8. In what timeframe have dissertations typically moved from start to defense?
9. When you think of your "best" chair experience, what did the student do that made it a positive experience?
10. Can you tell me about a difficulty you had on a committee as a chair and how it changed your approach to guiding dissertations?
11. What is your approach to dealing with dissention among the members of the committee?
12. What sorts of dissertations would you prefer not to chair?
13. In your experience, what are the most common stumbling blocks that students experience during the dissertation process?

Now add some other questions that you want to ask:

1. _____

_____

_____

2. _____

_____

_____

3. _____

_____

_____

Topic Cluster: Planning

The planning stage consists of all of the organization that you will do to make the dissertation "happen." This includes planning your time to complete the dissertation, planning for the cost involved in the dissertation, planning for the resources involved in completing the dissertation, and planning for risk management. During this stage, you will develop a schedule for your dissertation completion and you will focus on specific deliverables along the path of completion of the dissertation and assign completion dates for each. You will also need to assess the personal resources available to you to complete the dissertation, while addressing possible deficiencies. You should look at your budget for completing the dissertation—not only in terms of cost of schooling and the expense of the research but also in terms of the "cost" of time away from work or from family.

Topic: The Cost of the Dissertation

There are a variety of costs associated with the dissertation not only in terms of actual dollars spent, but also in terms of emotional costs. There is no argument that completing doctoral work and the dissertation is very costly. What makes it even costlier is that about half of the people who begin doctoral work never finish the dissertation—so they never see the benefits of having the Ph.D.

Financial Costs

It's important to state upfront that the vast majority of individuals who obtain a Ph.D. do not become wealthy because of that Ph.D. In fact, since most Ph.Ds. go into teaching—which is relatively low paying—they actually often earn less than individuals with Master's degrees and even many people with Bachelor's degrees. Most often, getting a Ph.D. is not done out of a motivation to simply make more money, but because individuals want to teach or conduct research. For many academic positions, it is—if not a requirement—then highly desirable.

To calculate the costs of your Ph.D., first add up the per-semester cost of tuition, less any grants than you may receive. Do not subtract the loans that you receive since these will need to be paid back (with interest). Keep in mind that during dissertation, some schools continue to charge per-semester tuition, while others charge only for a set number of dissertation credits (and some others charge a flat fee). These costs are fairly easy to calculate. There are also costs associated with not working a full-time job or part-time job—or continuing to work that job, but having to divide your time between the work you do at your job and the work you do on your dissertation.

Financial Cost Calculator for Coursework and Dissertation

1.	Cost of coursework (semester cost × number of semesters in coursework)	_____ × _____ = _____
2.	Cost of dissertation (**add** the flat fee or cost per semester)	_____ × _____ = _____
3.	Cost of not working (**subtract** the amount you make × number of years not working)	_____ × _____ = _____
4.	Cost of working less (**subtract** reduction in salary × years working less)	_____ × _____ = _____
5.	Calculation for actual cost of student loan (**add** loan amount + interest)	_____ + _____ = _____
6.	Living expenses (**add** rent, food, transportation × number of years in doctoral studies)	_____ × _____ = _____
7.	Grant monies and other monies that do not need to be paid back (**subtract** these!)	− _____
	Total	**$** _____

Obtaining funding. Obtaining some funding for your dissertation can help to alleviate the financial burden of the dissertation. There are four main sources of funding that you can pursue: stipends, fellowships, grants, and loans. A **stipend** is money that is given to you by your university or department in exchange for work; many doctoral students will receive stipends while they are pursuing coursework in exchange for assisting a professor with classes or research. A **teaching fellowship** is a position at your institution that prepares you to teach and pays a salary. A **research fellowship** does the same except you are conducting research. **Grants** are moneys that you can obtain from a variety of sources—including the federal government and private organizations—to support your research. Grants are not paid back. Most dissertation research is not grant funded, but that doesn't mean that you should not look into this option. There are grants available for particular research topics and also grants that are available to certain individuals—for example people of various descent, or veterans. Begin with a simple online search for grant sources. Some universities have an office that is established to help you obtain grant funding—be sure to check it out. **Loans** provide money that you borrow from a lender. These must be paid back—generally upon completion of your degree. Some loans will not accrue interest while you are still enrolled in school—others will. Be sure to consult with your university's office of financial aid to fully understand your loan obligations.

Emotional Costs

Calculating the emotional costs of the dissertation is very difficult. The Ph.D. process—like any schooling—is stressful. The dissertation is even more stressful because it requires that you conduct unique research. Completing a Ph.D. can cause stress-related illnesses and can take a toll on your mental health. You also must not discount the impact that completing your dissertation will have on your family. Many marriages and relationships suffer considerably—even to the point of breaking up. You may not be able to be involved in every activity at your children's school or go to all of their sporting events while working on your doctorate.

Dealing with the emotional costs can be more difficult than dealing with the financial costs of the dissertation. When examining financial costs, you may choose to limit the number of semesters you are in school to avoid paying more tuition, you can make an informed decision regarding the cost of tuition and choose a school that is reasonably priced, and you can take advantage of loans and grants available to help you pay for school. Dealing with emotional costs also requires some planning, but the key dealing with emotional costs is to be aware of them. Your family/spouse/significant other needs to be given time in your schedule in the same manner that the dissertation or your job is given time. Your children, other family, and friends need to be made aware that you will not be as available as you would be if you were not in school. They also need to know that the only way to finish your dissertation is to devote significant amounts of time to it. By engaging all the important people in your life in a dialogue about your schooling you can accomplish a number of goals: first, you let them know how important they are to you, simply by involving them in the conversation; second, they are forewarned that you will not be as available as you previously had been; third, this can start a conversation on how to carve out time to be with them that is meaningful, but will still allow you to devote enough time to school. Most importantly, by having this type of discussion upfront you are enlisting them to be part of your very important support network during this very stressful time. So, begin the conversations.

More serious emotional issues. There are also more serious emotional issues that can occur during your dissertation. The incidence of mental health problems in the college and graduate school population is very high. Some mental health problems may have been present in these individuals prior to graduate studies and simply became worse, while some may have only appeared during graduate studies. Graduate studies, by their nature, are highly stressful; you will be constantly tested and asked to stretch yourself. Some graduate students will experience significant mental health problems during their studies, but almost everyone experiences some type of personal issue during this time. Since graduate studies generally take 5-10 years to complete, the odds are that during that time some personal crisis or mental health issue will arise.

The types of mental health problems that may occur include depression, manic-depression, and anxiety. In extreme cases, some may feel aggressive, suicidal, or lose touch with reality. Individuals who are obsessive compulsive may have an advantage in their attention to detail, or they may never finish because they get lost in the very minute details. There are also a variety of symptoms that may occur or worsen during your dissertation: including weight gain or loss, fatigue, and difficulty concentrating.

Establishing a Baseline Questionnaire

Dealing with mental health problems begins with an awareness that these types of problems can occur and also an awareness of how you normally feel and behave. Wherever you are right now in your doctoral journey—whether you are already in the dissertation, or whether you are just beginning coursework—or haven't even been accepted yet—take a moment to reflect upon how you normally feel and behave.

Below is a list of 29 statements that will help you establish your baseline. Answer the questions on a separate sheet of paper, and then date and keep the paper. You can revisit this list often during your dissertation journey to check and see how you are doing.

1.	**I feel happy or at least neutral** Less than Usual Same as Usual More than Usual N/A
2.	**I have adequate time to get things done** Less than Usual Same as Usual More than Usual N/A
3.	**I feel depressed** Less than Usual Same as Usual More than Usual N/A
4.	**I prefer to be alone much of the time** Less than Usual Same as Usual More than Usual N/A
5.	**I sleep an adequate amount each night** Less than Usual Same as Usual More than Usual N/A
6.	**I worry a lot** Less than Usual Same as Usual More than Usual N/A
7.	**There is too much to do** Less than Usual Same as Usual More than Usual N/A
8.	**I like to be around people a lot** Less than Usual Same as Usual More than Usual N/A
9.	**I enjoy a number of activities other than school** Less than Usual Same as Usual More than Usual N/A

10.	**I am eating a healthy diet** Less than Usual Same as Usual More than Usual N/A
11.	**I am exercising** Less than Usual Same as Usual More than Usual N/A
12.	**I really do not have activities other than school in my life** Less than Usual Same as Usual More than Usual N/A
13.	**I have several close friends or family with whom I am in contact** Less than Usual Same as Usual More than Usual N/A
14.	**I really do not have close friends or family with whom I am in contact** Less than Usual Same as Usual More than Usual N/A
15.	**I am thinking of hurting myself or someone else** Less than Usual Same as Usual More than Usual N/A
16.	**I sometimes hear voices that aren't there** Less than Usual Same as Usual More than Usual N/A
17.	**I have stopped taking medications** Less than Usual Same as Usual More than Usual N/A
18.	**My weight has changed – it is…** Less than Usual Same as Usual More than Usual N/A
19.	**I feel as though I have difficulty breathing** Less than Usual Same as Usual More than Usual N/A
20.	**I feel as though the walls are closing in on me** Less than Usual Same as Usual More than Usual N/A
21.	**I can concentrate normally** Less than Usual Same as Usual More than Usual N/A
22.	**I am having trouble concentrating** Less than Usual Same as Usual More than Usual N/A
23.	**I take my vitamins** Less than Usual Same as Usual More than Usual N/A
24.	**I am drinking more than usual** Less than Usual Same as Usual More than Usual N/A
25.	**I am using drugs more than usual** Less than Usual Same as Usual More than Usual N/A
26.	**I feel good about my relationships with my spouse/significant other** Less than Usual Same as Usual More than Usual N/A
27.	**I feel good about my academic progress** Less than Usual Same as Usual More than Usual N/A
28.	**I know what is going on in my community** Less than Usual Same as Usual More than Usual N/A

Remember, this is not a diagnostic test, but merely a tool for you to use to be more aware about yourself. However, pay special attention to the items that can indicate serious difficulties (3, 6, 14, 15, 16, 17, 20 and 21). These are almost always a cause for concern. Most importantly, be alert for any drastic changes that occur—which may signal difficulties. All universities offer support for their students—if your problems become overwhelming, seek professional help at the university. There is no shame in asking for help—in fact, it can make you a much stronger person and provide you with excellent coping skills. Keep in mind that you do not have to wait until you have serious concerns before seeking the assistance of a professional. Counselors/therapists/life coaches can also help you become the best "you" that you can be!

Letting go of stress. It is not enough to merely be aware of how you normally behave and feel. You also need to have concrete plans for how you can cope with the stress that will come your way during the dissertation. Graduate school is inherently stressful—and you need to be able to function to the best of your ability. If you are feeling anxious and stressed out, you will not be able to concentrate well, and you will not be able to do your best work. You must be able to "de-stress."

De-stressing is a way of getting rid of stress or letting off steam: returning to your baseline. It can also be a way to improve upon your baseline. In some respects, de-stressing is also a way to escape from stress and pressures. There are many ways that you can decide to de-stress and some are better than others. Some will offer only a momentary escape from stress and can actually make your life worse in the long run (like excessive drug or alcohol use), and some may offer lasting benefits (like exercise or meditation).

When you select de-stressing activities, it may be beneficial to choose activities that are unlike any that you are performing for your dissertation. If your dissertation has you spending long hours on the computer, or reading many articles and books, or doing a significant amount of writing, then you may wish to choose de-stress activities that do not involve your computer or reading or writing. Sometimes just briefly getting away from those activities to which you have been devoting significant time can be relaxing and help you to de-stress. It can be very relaxing to just do something totally different—this can activate different areas of the brain and help you to see things in new ways.

Let's give some thought to how you can deal with not only the daily stress of the dissertation, but also those times where you may experience an acute stress crisis. Although there is some overlap, consider the following categories of activities when selecting your "de-stress" options:

- Exercise
- Hands-on
- Contemplative
- Interactive
- Do something different
- Use your mind a different way
- Clean up
- Pamper yourself
- Help others
- Think like a kid

You will see that many of the categories overlap and there are certainly other possible categories that could be added. The key here is that you are able to healthfully deal with your stress.

Exercise. Exercise is not only a viable way to de-stress, but you will also be rewarded with a physical pay-off in terms of being both healthier and in better shape. Exercise can be as simple as walking or swimming or yoga, or you can choose more strenuous forms of exercise like running, mountain biking, kick-boxing, karate, dancing, or tennis. While the benefit of being healthier and in better shape is a bonus, remember, the purpose for engaging in this activity while you are working on your dissertation is to lower your stress level.

Hands-on. When you choose an activity to de-stress with, you may want to choose something that allows you to be creative and hands-on: activities like cooking, knitting, sewing, woodworking, painting, refinishing furniture, and art (painting, sculpture, collages, coloring). It can be very fulfilling to engage in the act of creation and to see your finished results. These creative enterprises can provide further benefit by stimulating other areas of your brain.

Contemplative. You might want to consider something more contemplative when you choose a de-stressing activity. It can be very centering to engage in activities like journaling, writing, meditation, prayer, listening to music, or even simply walking in a park or down a quiet street. Focusing on your inner thoughts or feelings or on a belief in a higher being can really help make it clear what is important in your daily life and how to get past both small and large hurdles.

Interactive. It can also be very de-stressing to reach out and interact with others, such as communicating or interacting with friends, family, or a peer group. This can be through personal visits, phone calls, or email. You can invite people over for dinner, throw a big party, put together a cook-out—or accept invitations to such events if you have been passing them by. You may also want to consider joining a formal or informal support groups with other graduate students where you can complain, vent, or discuss issues in a safe environment. Also, don't overlook the benefits of interaction with a pet, whether it be walking your dog or taking care of a tank full of tropical fish, these activities can help you de-stress.

Do something different. De-stressing can be a matter of getting out and doing something different from your normal routine. Go somewhere that serves really good coffee or tea—perhaps some authentic Indian Chai? Visit an amusement park or haunted house. Take a tour of something local. Go for a drive, or to a festival, or fair. Go on a hike. Visit a museum, art gallery, observatory or arboretum.

Use your mind a different way. While it may seem somewhat counter-intuitive to suggest using your mind even more than you are right now, using it in a very different way can not only help you alleviate stress but it can also provide you with fresh perspective when you do return to your dissertation work. Consider working your mind in a different way, for example through puzzles or games—such as online gaming, board games, poker night, or limited sessions of playing games on your phone.

Clean up. Although it may not seem to be the case, it can actually be relaxing and de-stressing to clean! This is because it gives you immediate control and you see a very quick payoff. Clean a room or even a junk drawer. Organize something you collect. Get rid of all of your recycling or go through that pile of mail and catalogs that has been stacking up. You may also see a payoff when you return to work—many people do work better in a clean and organized environment.

Pamper yourself. Of course, in any time of great stress, like the dissertation, you should be sure to pamper yourself—just be careful that you do not spend a lot of money if your financial resources are tight or stretched. There are numerous options that are free or low cost: Take a long bath with bubbles or salts, read a book for fun, do not set the alarm clock and allow yourself to sleep in late, watch bad reality shows for a whole afternoon. If you have some extra cash, you might want to consider getting a massage or manicure or even going away for a day or weekend—if you can afford a little mini-vacation every once in a while, it can be a great help and help to reset your internal stress-meter!

Help others. It may seem like more stress to start adding to your to-do list by helping others, but carefully chosen volunteer work can actually be very relaxing and rewarding. Your involvement doesn't need to lead to a huge time commitment. Collect donations for your favorite charity. Volunteer some time and work at the food bank. Or work with the elderly, the sick or with young children. When the dissertation asks so much of us, giving a little to others can refresh you. It can also make us thankful that we have so much and also have the opportunity to pursue the highest degree awarded by academia.

Think like a kid. One way to de-stress is to go back to the things that you loved as a child—a time for many of us where there were far fewer stressors! For you, this might be something you did as a young child—like pickup baseball or frisbee, or something you did while in college—like going to that artsy cinema to watch foreign movies. As children, we didn't need to de-stress because we intuitively knew how to make ourselves feel better. Try this again.

Avoid the harmful. There are also some ways to de-stress that can have very negative consequences like drinking to excess, taking a lot of drugs, shopping excessively, eating too much, engaging in co-dependent relationship or engaging in sex with random partners. While each of these can serve as an escape—each also carries with it the potential for harmful consequences. You don't want the price of your escape to be a lifelong addiction. When you choose a way to de-stress, make healthy choices that will also benefit you in the long run. The demands of doctoral studies and the dissertation create significant imbalance in your life by focusing so much effort on only one portion of our lives. What you choose as your methods of de-stressing should help you lead a happy and healthy life; you must make choices that will keep your life in balance

Topic: Time Management

In order to get any task done, time management—or how you allocate and plan your schedule and priorities—is a necessity. Even if you have plenty of time, it is important to employ time management techniques so that you do not become overly distracted by other tasks. For a significant task, such as a dissertation, time management is a necessity.

The entire dissertation project can seem daunting and insurmountable, but if you break it down into smaller components—more easily manageable tasks—you can move through it more effectively and even reward yourself for achieving specific significant milestones. Part of time management is also determining *what* you are managing, and then allocating the proper amount of days or weeks or months for that task based on how long you believe it will take you,

Most of us have a limited amount of time available to us in which we must complete the dissertation. Even if we are lingering in our program in order to delay repaying student loans, everyone wants—and needs—to get done. Being in doctoral studies can feel like you are putting your life on hold. The grad student life can be enjoyable, but only for a while: everyone eventually gets tired of the low level of pay that a teaching fellow earns—particularly when you see full-time faculty making at least double what you are making. In the current academic world—where the number of non-traditional students pursuing advanced degrees is growing at a rapid rate—many students who are attempting to finish a dissertation also have other obligations that are clamoring for their attention. If you are a "non-traditional" graduate student—meaning that you did not pursue all of your degrees prior to entering the workforce; you returned to schooling after a significant time off; you have a job; you have a family—then time management is absolutely crucial to you. You need to set boundaries and achievable goals in order to complete your dissertation. Even among many "traditional" graduate students, by the time you are at the dissertation point of doctoral studies, you may now be married, have children, be teaching in your department or at another school, or even working a non-related job simply to help support yourself and/or your family. Regardless of whether the time pressure may be a result of the expense, or stress, or time taken away from work or family, it is a tangible motivating factor to finish the dissertation in as timely and efficient a manner as possible. Good time management becomes an absolute necessity if each semester you are in dissertation is expensive in terms of tuition—or in terms of time lost from working, or lost from being engaged with your family or significant other. Maybe you are running out of loans and need to finish before you run out of money, or you need the degree completed for a promotion at work, to keep your job, or even to get a job; these can be strong motivating factors to push you to finish as quickly as possible. If you feel that your schooling is keeping you disengaged from your family or even from enjoying your life, you may feel that a quick, efficient, well-written dissertation is the best dissertation.

Time management is a matter of establishing priorities for tasks and committing the necessary time to complete these tasks, but it is also important to determine how you can work best (this will be discussed later). For many of the reasons stated above, the dissertation simply must be a priority. For the non-traditional student, of course, family and work are also competing priorities, but if the dissertation is always placed at the bottom of your "to-do list," it will never get done. This means that you must commit time frequently to working on the dissertation.

In order for an 18-month or twelve-month dissertation timeline to be viable and to work, there is a tremendous amount of prep-work that you need to do. This prep work includes the following:

1. Have your topic selected (and make sure it represents a gap in the literature)
2. Conduct the majority of your literature review
3. Consider the feasibility of your study with regard to time and finances
4. Consider the feasibility of your subject selection (e.g.: CEOs and medical doctors are unlikely to have the time or inclination to participate in research)
5. Consider any site permissions that you may require to conduct your research (e.g., from a state department of education if you will be doing research in a high school)
6. If you are using secondary data, you must locate that dataset and confirm access to it prior to beginning the dissertation.

To create your timeline for what you need to get done, first determine when you want to have a project finished and then work your way backward from that point. Since the dissertation is such a large project, set mini goals such as:

- Writing the literature review.
- Writing the proposal.
- Getting through IRB.
- Data collection.
- Data analysis.
- Writing the final document.
- Final editing.

Your initial attempt at a timeline may be unrealistic—especially if you do not have ways to double-check that you are meeting your goals. If you are going to complete your literature review in a month, what needs to be done by the end of this week? What needs to be done by the end of today? If data collection will take you two months, from how many subjects do you need to obtain data each week? And, of course, there is the element of the unknown that will pop up when you are at any point in the dissertation. Ask almost anyone who has completed a dissertation and they will tell you that somewhere during the process, something happened; some stumbling block came up that they needed to navigate around. For example, what happens if you discover as you conduct your literature review that a study exactly like yours has already been done? What happens if the site where you wanted to collect data will not give you permission to do so? What if you cannot recruit enough subjects? What if your qualitative interview questions are not yielding the rich responses they were intended to? What if you become ill? What if you lose your job? What if you divorce? There are many possible delays and stumbling blocks in research and it is not always possible to predict or prepare for all of them, but you should be aware of as many of them as possible—and create alternate plans for everything. As we always tell students: "have a Plan B, Plan C, and Plan D for everything." Finishing a dissertation is very much like disaster planning: prepare for the worst but hope for the best.

Let's create a sample timeline. The twelve-month or 18-month timeline is premised on three factors:

First, that you have done a lot of legwork on your dissertation topic while you were doing your coursework (this is one of the benefits of reading this book as you begin your doctoral studies). You will have spent much of your time in coursework writing and working on a draft of the first three chapters of your proposal. Of course, this will not be set in stone until your committee approves your proposal, but having prepared chapter 2 (generally the literature review) and chapter 3 (methodology) ahead of time will really allow you to hit the proverbial ground running.

Second, you need to know when your school's Institutional Review Board (IRB) meets and, if it requires changes to your proposal, how long the wait will be until it meets again (especially if your research will require a "full review"—we will discuss more on the IRB process later). At some schools, if you miss the date for submitting IRB materials you may wait *months* for them to meet again; at other schools, the IRB meets only once per semester. You definitely want to know its meeting date(s) ahead of time so that you can plan accordingly. Here, timing is everything!

Third, it is assumed that you are working on your dissertation full-time. This means approximately 40 hours each week. Even if you have a full-time job, you should also consider the dissertation a full-time job as well. It takes a lot of work and time to conduct unique research and write it up, and you must devote time accordingly. If you are only working on your dissertation part-time, you will need to at *least* double the timeline. You should also be aware that this timeline is premised upon you having a strong writing ability and having good research skills and academic preparation.

If you are missing one of these three key factors, don't despair. While this makes an 18-month dissertation less likely, you can still complete in a reasonable amount of time. If you have not done any prep work, build 6 more months onto the timeline to do that prep work. If you are not going to be working full-time on the dissertation, then you will have to expand the timeframe accordingly. If you devote 20 hours each week to the dissertation, 36 months is more reasonable.

Sample 18-Month Timeline

You will notice that this timeline does not work out to exactly 18 months. It is very difficult to estimate how long different school processes will take. The time estimates given here are minimal and assume that you are working on your dissertation full time. You should also build in 3-6 months for unexpected challenges along the way.

	Quantitative	Qualitative
Literature review (Chapter 2)	complete a draft prior to beginning the dissertation	
Chapters 1 & 3	complete a draft prior to beginning the dissertation	
Finalize Chapter 2	1 month	1 month
Finalize Chapter 3	1 month	1 month
Finalize Chapter 1	1 month	1 month
IRB	varies depending upon school (average 1 semester)	
Data Collection	1 month*	3-6 months**
Data Analysis	1 month	2 months
Writing Chapter 4	1 month	2 months
Writing Chapter 5	1 month	1 month
Redrafting	1 month	2 months

School processes	varies depending upon school
Dissertation defense	varies depending upon school

* Longer if there are problems obtaining subjects
** Shorter when you use secondary data

Topic: Working Conditions

In order to complete the dissertation, you must determine how you work best. This doesn't mean that you should wait for the perfect time to work, but rather you need to know how to create the environment that will allow you to get your work done in the best possible manner.

Ask yourself the following questions:

1. "Do I need quiet to work?"
2. "Do I need large blocks of time to work?"
3. "Do I need to be alone to work?"
4. "What time of day do I work best?"
5. "Where can I do my best work?"
6. "Do I Need Quiet to Work?"

Some people really need to be in a quiet location to be able to focus and to think and write—while other people prefer background noise, such as music. Personally, I (O'Reilly) usually like to work with the television on and I don't like too much quiet. I actually wrote large portions of my dissertation while sitting in a local *Chuck E. Cheese*'s with my young, twin daughters. If you need quiet, you need to ask yourself if you can have the quiet you need at home. If a quiet location is essential to you and you do not have that at home, then a local library can be a good place to work—whether it is at your doctoral institution or the public library.

"Do I Need Large Blocks of Time to Work?"

To complete a dissertation you must set aside ample time to work. Data collection can be time consuming, especially in a qualitative dissertation, or if you have difficulty recruiting subjects. Your schedule may not allow you to devote large blocks of working time each day because of other commitments; an alternative to devoting large blocks of time each day is to work in "microbursts." Microbursts are short periods of time that you devote to very concentrated and focused work. Microbursts require that you plan your work because there is no time to be thinking about what you need to do, you just need to do it; they can be scheduled in between other work that you do. Even now, I (O'Reilly) often schedule microbursts of work between other activities—such as cooking, cleaning and my professional and academic writing. A word of caution: some people are able to do this— some cannot. I enjoy working in microbursts and, in fact, I can get more work done when I schedule a variety of tasks. This is an ideal technique for people who find it difficult to work an extended period of time, who do not have extended blocks of time to work in, or who find that their focus wanders. You will need to take this into consideration with your time management and timeline creation.

"Do I Need to be Alone to Work?"

Some people cannot work with the distraction of having other people around. Others only find people they know to be distracting and are able to work efficiently in a crowded space as long as they have no one with whom they need to engage. Still others can work in the same room as other family members or friends as long as everyone is working quietly. Some people find it very lonely to work without other people around. What is your ideal? If you have an office in your home, you might want to work there; if you have an office at your doctoral institution, you might want to mostly work there.

"What Time of Day Do I Work Best?"

Some people work best in the morning, others work best in the afternoon, and then others at night. When writing a dissertation, you probably won't have the luxury of only working at the "best time" for you. To a certain extent, you'll have to suck it up and learn to work as often as possible. But, if you are setting aside planned blocks of time to work, and you work best in the mornings, if at all possible, schedule your dissertation time for mornings. Although I'm certainly not a morning person, I (O'Reilly) have learned that I usually do my best creative work—and that includes writing—in the morning, first thing, while my mind is clear and before I've become bogged down with all of the details and minutiae of the day ahead. Also give some thought to scheduling tasks for times when you can do them best. While you may do your best writing in the morning, perhaps you can devote afternoons to reading. Or might you do your writing in the morning and editing later in the day? You will also need to set aside time each week to assess your progress so that you stay on track.

"Where Can I Do My Best Work?"

There is no ideal place where everyone can do their best work. Everyone is different. I (O'Reilly) once owned a house and it was the only time I had a dedicated office, and in my beautiful office, where I could look out of the window at the palm trees (this was in Florida), I had a great desk for my computer and my files and some books. It looked absolutely wonderful, but I never did a lick of work there. I don't know why—it was ideal—but it just wasn't conducive to my focus and work style. It wasn't long before I converted the room into a playroom for my daughters. They got tons of use out of the room and loved their "Little Tykes" desks, whereas, I couldn't tear myself away from the living room sofa, in front of the TV, with all my books and papers and computer piled on the end table beside me where I diligently cranked through my work. I have never changed from that set-up; occasionally, when I find home too distracting or I need to get some new ideas for creative work, I escape that environment and go to a coffee shop.

Consider whether or not you will be able to work with the distractions of home. Will you find yourself constantly side-tracked by your significant other, spouse, children, pets, or neighbors? Will undone household tasks nag at you and prevent you from doing your best work? It is common for people to work at coffee shops—this gets you out of the house and away from distractions, but it will also cost you money in terms of buying cups of coffee. The public library (or a university library) is another good choice for a place to work but may be constrained by the facility's operating schedule. If you hold a full-time job, you may have the option of doing your writing there. We have known many faculty members who were already working as full-time professors while they were completing the dissertation—working during the office hours that they must keep for students. You have to be in your office anyhow, and very few students tend to actually utilize their professors' office hours. Some people stay after-hours at their workplace and dedicate that time to their dissertation. Determine where you can do your best work and be mindful that you may need to change that location from time to time to keep your creative juices flowing.

Be Wary of the "Perfect Working Conditions" Trap

Be careful not to allow yourself to fall into the "perfect working conditions" trap: the thought that you must have the perfect office, a clean desk, perfect quiet, long blocks of time, etc. This alone can be a way of sabotaging your success. When you ask yourself what you need to work, also ask yourself what is realistic. While you may feel that you need large blocks of time to work, if that doesn't seem likely, you'll have to adjust to less than ideal conditions. This is significantly better than not working at all. If you want to work in quiet but have three children at home and must work at home, you may not be able to always have the quiet you need. You will need to learn to adjust and find a way to make it work or—plain and simple—you will not be able to succeed. Realizing this is vitally important: the conditions may rarely be "ideal," but they can be workable. If you find yourself not being able to get those conditions in place that you feel you need to work, you may need to just "make do" and work in less than perfect conditions. One thing that will predict your success in the dissertation is how adaptable you can be—to changes requested by your committee, to demands made on you in collecting data, and to working in less than ideal working conditions.

Working Conditions Checklist

Now complete the following checklist to determine how you work best, then determine how likely it is that you can create these "best" working conditions, and whether or not you "must" have each of those conditions to work.

1.   Do I need quiet to work?   Yes   Sometimes   No

      Is it likely that I can get this condition?

      Can I work without this?

2.   Do I need large blocks of time to work?   Yes   Sometimes   No

      Is it likely that I can get this condition?

      Can I work without this?

3.   Do I need to be alone to work?   Yes   Sometimes   No

      Is it likely that I can get this condition?

      Can I work without this?

4.   What time of day do I work best?   _____

      Is it likely that I can get this condition?

      Can I work without this?

5.   Where can I do my best work?   _____

      Is it likely that I can get this condition?

      Can I work without this?

Now, from the Working Conditions Checklist, determine which factors you cannot work without and maximize your opportunities to work under those conditions. If you need to rearrange your life for a while, do it. The key here is to work with what you have or create what you can—and then to accept your working conditions as the most ideal that they can be—and to dive in and begin the tasks at hand.

Topic: Distractions and Setting Priorities

We could finish the dissertation if we could maintain a singular focus in our lives and work very hard every day, but there are hundreds of possible reasons for not working—and not finishing your dissertation. Life will constantly get in the way of finishing the dissertation—even for the traditional student who is not working and does not have a family. You should expect that there will be other things going on in your life, but it is important that you not make excuses. Whenever something unexpected happens that forces you to take a break or calls your attention away from your work, you need to deal with the distraction and then return to your dissertation work as soon as possible.

If you do not have time to work on your dissertation, it is you who are responsible for that lack of time. It is because of decisions that you have made or enabled, and the priorities that you have set. In order to have enough time to work on the dissertation, you must *make the time*. It is important that you recognize that others aren't to blame. When you get side-tracked, it is because you have allowed yourself to get side-tracked, and it is up to you to get yourself back on track. This doesn't mean you should get lost in self-recrimination because of time you've spent doing other things. It means that you should accept what has happened and then get yourself back on course.

To finish your dissertation you must be very clear about what your priorities are. If you have a job and a family, those are priorities, yet the dissertation must also be a priority. Sometimes the family must come first, sometimes the job must come first, but sometimes the dissertation must come first. One way to set priorities is to approach the dissertation the same way you would a job—because you should think of it as a job. Set aside time each day to work on the dissertation, several hours at least. Establish a place where you work on your dissertation every day. Ideally you will approach the dissertation like you would any other job—and devote eight hours a day, five days a week to completing it. By making your dissertation part of a routine, you can guarantee that your work on it will advance the project in a steady manner. But just as you occasionally take a vacation day so that work does not become monotonous, it is acceptable—and healthy—to reward yourself with an occasional break, or day off, from your dissertation. Consider making such days "rewards" for reaching certain milestones in your dissertation plan.

Beyond making the dissertation one of your top priorities, you need to be able to efficiently deal with all of the distractions that will arise and can get in your way of working on the dissertation. It is important to face the fact that we all have distractions in our lives—things that keep us from doing what we know we need to do. If you find yourself playing games on your phone or texting, or doing housework or watching television as opposed to working during periods of time allotted for your dissertation, you very likely are allowing yourself to be distracted. Giving into distractions is a way of procrastinating. We all give into distraction sometimes. When the creative process is going well, these little breaks, in moderation, actually help me work better and faster—but that is my personal working style. There will always be distractions. Some students will do the bulk of their work in the early morning hours, or only work at the library, or at a coffeehouse—all in an effort to combat the distractions they find the most diverting. What you must be on the lookout for is when the distractions really become a way of procrastinating—of not getting your dissertation done. We are often distracted with activities that are easier or more fun than what we know we must accomplish. Playing games on my phone is fun, doing housework is easy—but both can prevent me from finishing my work in a timely fashion.

List of Distractions

Below is a list of common distractions that students encounter during the dissertation phase of their doctoral work. Check off the items that are the main distractions for you and then add others at the end of the list.

1. Emailing/texting friends
2. Playing electronic games (on the computer, the TV, or your phone)
3. Eating (snacking)
4. Spouse or significant other
5. Family, including children and pets
6. Friends
7. Drinking and partying
8. Working a full time job
9. Hobbies
10. _____
11. _____
12. _____

In all fairness, while all of these things can be distractions, many of them are also important parts of your life—like your significant other, your family and friends or your job. They can also be ways that you choose to de-stress. Yet, at times, each item on this list, no matter how important or trivial, can also serve as a distraction: You should return friends' emails; helping your children with their homework is important; playing online games can be relaxing. Please don't misunderstand we are not suggesting that you ignore your friends' emails, or not help your children with homework or give up online games—you need to establish which must be done, which are priorities, and which should be relegated to certain times—like after you have completed your dissertation work for the day. For example, after two hours of work, you can deal with emails—or turn your phone back on—if those are among your distractions. Perhaps your spouse or another family member can pitch in and help your children with their homework.

The key to combating distractions is to know that they exist and which ones you are most likely to encounter—and to have a plan for how to combat the distractions, and know how you will get back on track—following those times when the distractions do get the best of you. Now that you have created your list, it's time to plan how to deal with them. Ultimately, you have full control over the distractions in your life—but in some cases, other people play a significant role in those distractions. Dealing with them will require setting boundaries and managing the expectations of others by not making excuses, communicating priorities, and accepting responsibility—many of the topics that we covered in this cluster.

Now ask yourself, "How am I going to deal with each of these distractions?" Family must be a priority, but every family member must also know that your degree is important and they need to respect that—the same way that you may respect your children's love of hockey or soccer and take them to their games. You are in a great position to set a good example for your children or siblings about the importance of education. The best way to deal with any distraction is to have a plan. Some distractions can be used as motivation—for example, if you just love playing games on your phone, use it as reward for finishing an hour's worth of work or a day's worth of work. In some cases, you might want to ask someone else to take care of the distraction for you—like having your spouse take care of helping with homework three nights each week. Some distractions you might need to give up for a while—others might need to be indulged in only once a week or once a month.

Make a list of your top five biggest distractions, and include two different ways to deal with each:

1. _____

   _____

   a. I will deal with this distraction by_____

   _____

   b. Or by _____

   _____

2. _____

   _____

   a. I will deal with this distraction by_____

   _____

   b. Or by_____

   _____

3. _____

   _____

   a. I will deal with this distraction by_____

   _____

   b. Or by_____

   _____

4. _____

   _____

   a. I will deal with this distraction by_____

   _____

   b. Or by_____

   _____

5. _____

   _____

   a. I will deal with this distraction by _____

   _____

   b. Or by_____

   _____

Finally, if you do become distracted, don't waste time of self-recriminations. We all get distracted sometime—just get back to work and realize that sometimes we become distracted when we need to take a little break, so it's okay to take a day off from time to time or stop working early and maybe enjoy a nice sunset or an evening with friends, your significant other, or your children.

Topic: Content Area Preparation

A certain amount of academic preparation is required prior to setting out to write the dissertation proposal, completing your research and writing the dissertation. This academic preparation generally encompasses three areas: content-area preparation, research preparation, and writing preparation.

For the vast majority of individuals who set out to write a dissertation, content-area knowledge is commonly the least problematic of the three academic areas. Much of your coursework should have focused on your content area, as have many of the papers you have written at the doctoral level. There can be certain challenges in content area knowledge, however. One is if you have been working in the field prior to or during working on your doctoral degree. When you work in the field you acquire *practical* knowledge of the field, but that knowledge must be separated from *academic* knowledge of the field; practical knowledge can taint your writing and bias your research and conclusions. Academic knowledge stems purely from a research basis—which is very broad and takes into account the experiences of many individuals, whereas practical knowledge stems from your own personal experiences—which tend to be more limited. On the other hand, students who have never worked in the field are often missing a connection to the real-world application of what is being investigated in research. They have seen the research side, but have not seen these things put into practice. A balance of these experiences is ideal, with the recognition of the need to compartmentalize any opinions or biases that you may have so that the academic research you conduct stands entirely on its own merit.

It should be stressed that coursework alone is not enough to prepare you for working with your topic in your dissertation. Coursework presents a background in the general subject area of your dissertation. The courses you have taken will have provided an understanding of the basics of the discipline—but writing a dissertation is not about the basics. It is about taking the foundation from your coursework and building upon it so that you will become the expert in that small piece of your field. To do this, the real key is to read everything you can get your hands on—or download to your computer.

Your best friend throughout your doctoral studies—and especially throughout your dissertation—is definitely your librarian. Whether you go to a physical library or use the services of an electronic library, the librarian will help you find all of the buried treasure of academic literature.

Let's talk about the beauty of the library. Libraries are no longer musty old buildings filled with dusty books—often their most precious tools are not even housed within a building. They, like much of the rest of our lives are highly digitized and provide access to many, many databases. Libraries have evolved tremendously in the past two decades, with much of their catalog now available online.

It's a good idea to talk early and often with a librarian about any research that you are doing—even if it seems to be going well. Your librarian can provide you with searching skills and ways of organizing your results that will serve your well throughout your academic career.

Tricks from the Library

While there are many tricks you may learn from your librarian, I've selected some of my own favorites to include here:

Seminal works. In order to do any literature review properly, you must know what the seminal works are in your topic or discipline. Seminal works are very important pieces of literature that have changed the discipline or moved the discipline forward in very important ways—for example Sigmund Freud's "Interpretation of Dreams" in the field of psychology. They will be frequently cited in other literature in your discipline. While most of your literature review will be focused on very recent literature (the last five years or so), seminal works may be more dated, but are still salient to your topic. Make sure you know the seminal works in your topic area and always use them to place your dissertation work in the context of the broader literature.

Bibliography mining and cited reference searching. Bibliographic mining and cited reference searching are related techniques. You begin with a really great article and from that article you review all of the articles that it cites in its reference section. Then, you take that really great article and find articles that have been published more recently than it which cite it as a source. This helps you to see an arc of the literature and can be a great way to find many articles related to your topic (and also many authors who do work in your topic area).

Reference or citation management software. These software tools are a great way to organize your references for your dissertation or for any other academic writing you are doing. Once you put your references into the software you can use them over and over for any writing that you do which utilizes the same articles. It makes it a lot easier than having to re-create your reference list each time you write a paper or an article.

Author and journal notifications. Many academic libraries offer you the service of receiving author and journal notifications as long as you are a registered student. To set up journal notifications, let the librarian know what journals you are interested in (and there should be several), and you will receive an email notification with a link to the journal every time a new issue becomes available. Author notifications are similar; you will be notified every time important authors to your dissertation publish something new.

Topic: Research Preparation

The most frequent "missing piece" of academic preparation for doctoral students is the category of research preparation. Everyone who has advanced to the dissertation phase of their academic career has done academic writing, and has worked on a variety of topics in their discipline. The dissertation is unique research that you must design, conduct, and then write about. Some programs prepare students very well for this task. We have known doctoral students—especially those in the biological sciences—who will spend their entire doctoral careers in laboratories: first helping with experiments (including the daily running of them) and taking measurements, and then writing them up for presentation at conferences or for publication; then they will move on to more autonomous roles in these laboratories, choosing an area to research and conducting their own experiments—these experiments then become the basis of their own dissertations. Lucky them: they are very well prepared to tackle the dissertation. Some schools will offer work positions to their graduate students that include helping professors to conduct research. In the social sciences, such positions are common, although many graduate students opt instead to work in the area of teaching, which prepares them for the teaching side of a university career; teaching positions, however, do little to prepare them for the research portion of the dissertation, or for a research career. Other schools offer ample opportunities for students to work under a faculty member who is doing research—some from the undergraduate level upward. You should also have completed coursework in research; it is a good idea to have coursework in both quantitative and qualitative research methods, as well as in statistics. Remember that your coursework is preparing you to understand research. In many fields, this requires an understanding of both quantitative and qualitative research—even though many fields conduct limited qualitative research.

Research Preparedness Questionnaire

Take a moment to think about your research training up until this point. Look at the following list and determine which exposure to research you have had, and which you lack:

1.	Worked under a research faculty member as an undergraduate	Yes	No
2.	Worked under a research faculty member at the master's level	Yes	No
3.	Was actively involved in publishing/presenting research at the master's level	Yes	No
4.	Worked under a research faculty member at the doctoral level	Yes	No
5.	Actively involved in publishing/presenting research at the doctoral level	Yes	No
6.	Have taken a course in qualitative research	Yes	No
7.	Have taken more than one course in qualitative research	Yes	No
8.	Have taken a course in quantitative research	Yes	No
9.	Have taken more than one course in quantitative research	Yes	No
10.	Have taken a statistics course	Yes	No
11.	Have taken more than one statistics course	Yes	No

If you answered with many "yes" responses, you are probably well prepared. If you answered with many "no" responses, this helps you know where some of your weaknesses lie. If you are taking this Research Preparedness Questionnaire early in your doctoral career, you may want to arrange courses or learning opportunities to address any weaknesses that this has revealed. Keep in mind; the dissertation process is a learning experience, so you are not expected to be a seasoned researcher. This is where you learn how to be a researcher.

Research Tips and Tricks

The dissertation is about unique research. Research, by its nature, is a process—the dissertation is merely the write-up of that research. The process of research begins with your review of previous research (the literature review) upon which you build your own study. After you have completed the dissertation and it is published (as all dissertations are), others will build new research upon what you have done.

The research log. The research log is a tool that can help you organize the research that you do; it will help to make the research more useful to you in your daily work. I (Mink) used the paper version of the research log when I was working on my dissertation, but, of course, electronic versions are frequently used now—I'll bet there's even an app for that!

The research log should include all of the information that you need for your references. It will also include a brief summary of the research. It's a good idea to use some sort of spreadsheet program to create your log and use at least the following columns: author, date published, title, journal name if it is an article, theory, methods, design, findings, and notes.

Author	Date published	Title	Journal name	Theories used	Method used	Design used	Major findings	Notes

Of course, this is just an example—work with it for a while and you can add the columns that you need to best assist you in tracking your research. This will help you conduct all three types of literature review (topic, methodological, theoretical—which we will discuss later). When you are reading so much it can be difficult to keep track of it all—the research log provides a shorthand way of being able to see all of the important parts of the literature that you have reviewed.

The dissertation journal. Keeping a dissertation journal can assist you in a variety of ways during the process of writing the dissertation (you will recall that we discussed journaling as one of the ways you can choose to de-stress). The dissertation journal was born out of three separate concepts—"Morning Pages" from Julia Cameron's *The Artist's Way*, "field notes" made popular in the qualitative research tradition, and the "dissertation process journal" which focuses on the nuts and bolts process and what happens during the creation of the dissertation.

Morning pages and the traditional journal. The concept of "Morning Pages" made popular by Julia Cameron in her series of books about writing (*The Artist's Way*, see RESOURCES for others). She recommends to writers that they write three pages each morning to get the "noise" out of their heads—and by "noise" she means everything and anything—complaints, grocery lists, stream-of-consciousness, everything that is inside. By getting the inside out on paper, it clears the mind to focus on the writing task at hand—in your case—the dissertation. This is a way of priming the writing pump. If you engage, each morning, in the act of writing, it will get you into the habit of writing and you will write more and you will write better.

You can look at this also much like a traditional journal where you record your thoughts and feelings each morning before beginning the business of your day. It can also be a place for you to air your grievances. If you write down all of your complaints or problems it will give you control over them and they will not seem as overwhelming. You can also start to brainstorm about the best ways to deal with your grievances. If something is bothering you—get it out!

Qualitative field notes. The concept of the field journal comes from the qualitative research tradition, and is an integral part of the research. If you are conducting a qualitative dissertation, you may already be keeping a field journal. Qualitative researchers may use Field notes as a form of data collection in their research, but this is also a place for them to bring to the surface their biases and what they see emerging from the research. If you are writing a qualitative dissertation, this sort of writing might be used in your data analysis.

The dissertation process journal. The dissertation process journal allows you to mull over the process of writing the dissertation. It can help you decide what is working for you—and what is not. You can use it as a place to sort through the many pieces of the dissertation, and write about your literature review strategy, for instance, or discuss with yourself the benefits of different methods of data collection. Use it to plan your work and to brainstorm for ideas about how to make the process easier. While the morning pages is just about getting everything out of your head, the process journal is about giving yourself a place to work with and reflect on the dissertation process.

Topic: Writing Preparation

Writing preparation not only means that you can write a well-structured English sentence/paragraph/chapter, but also that you can write in the style necessary to complete a dissertation—which is very different from almost any other writing you will ever do. This writing style has similarities to other academic writing, but even that is a different animal. So while you might be able to write a good paper—or even a book, like the one you are reading—these writing skills do not necessarily translate into the realm of writing a dissertation. It certainly is helpful to be a good writer, but other than the mechanics of putting together a sentence or paragraph, good dissertation writing is more about being able to follow a formula for writing and it is a formula that contains a lot of repetition.

When you are writing the dissertation you are, in effect, writing a book. This can be very daunting—just thinking about it strikes fear in the hearts of many doctoral students. The vast majority of individuals who start doctoral studies but who do not earn the degree drop out at some point during the dissertation. Most doctoral students have not written a book—or contributed chapters to a book previously—so writing the dissertation can be quite a task. However, a dissertation and a book share little in common aside from length, as a dissertation is unique in structure and style. And that's something to be kept in mind: the dissertation is not like other writing—it is not even like writing academic articles. It is a very repetitive and stilted way of writing. Being forewarned is akin to being armed for dealing with the dissertation beast.

Go to the UMI Dissertation Abstracts database and look at some of the dissertations from your institution. Notice how many of the chapter subheadings are similar. Notice how repetitive the dissertation seems to be. It seems to keep saying the same thing over and over—this is to walk the reader through the research that was conducted. You may find a similar style in some academic journals—however, it is usually less repetitive. Dissertations also will most often contain standardized sections that are not necessarily included in every academic journal article. Dissertations must clearly build a bridge from previous research, and they must contain theory. Dissertations must also include suggestions for future research.

There are a variety of ways to make this writing easier. This chapter will focus on the following writing tips:

1. Having a writing critique
2. The dissertation manual
3. The appropriate style manual
4. Focusing on the purpose of each chapter—and writing them separately
5. Aligning all of your chapters
6. Separating your writing process from your editing process
7. Never wait for inspiration; be the inspiration
8. The reverse outline
9. Setting a daily (or 5 days a week) schedule and writing goal and sticking to it
10. What about the stuff you write that you don't use?

Having a Writing Critique

Make sure that you can, in fact, write. Don't assume that because you've written papers for courses that you can actually write a dissertation. Have an honest analysis of your writing conducted. Many universities have Writing Centers or other services that will be happy to provide you with an honest critique of your writing; take advantage of this early—and often.

Anyone who has written a book or article knows that editors tear apart work that is submitted—so don't be put off by someone who may be a harsh critic of your writing. A key factor in getting through the dissertation is being able to take constructive criticism without taking it personally. So get that sort of feedback for your writing, and get it early in your doctoral career. Then you can adapt your style for successful academic writing. Be sure that you know proper grammar, usage, and mechanics—and remember—clarity is key.

The Dissertation Manual

First, if your University does not have a dissertation manual, do yourself a favor and read a number of dissertations produced by your department; take note of the subheadings and layout, if nothing else. Although there are numerous reasons for you to read the dissertations from your school, some of the most important are:

- Acquaints you with what various chairs view as acceptable
- Allows you to see a variety of styles of dissertation writing
- Lets you know what topics are commonly pursued in your department
- Gives you an understanding of whether or not both quantitative and qualitative research is conducted in your department

Appropriate Style Manual

Along with your school's dissertation manual, you should have a copy of the appropriate style manual for your department. There are quite literally dozens of style manuals, but the most common are APA and MLA. You should consult the style manual used in your program and employ its guidelines in all of your doctoral-level writing. The more comfortable you become with the style manual early on, the easier it will be for you to complete the writing of the dissertation—and you do not want to be consulting a style manual when writing each paragraph while you are coping with the huge task of writing your dissertation.

Focusing on the Purpose of Each Chapter—and Writing Them Separately

Focus on the purpose of each chapter and write each separately. For the proposal, we would recommend writing chapters 2 (literature review) and 3 (methodology), then writing chapter 1, which serves as the introduction. Likewise, for the dissertation, go back and rewrite chapter 1 last, incorporating everything that has been done since the proposal.

Aligning all of Your Chapters

Make sure that there is alignment among your chapters—this can be as simple as the theory that you mention in chapter 1 is the theory that you cover in depth in chapter 2, and is, in fact, the theory that you are using to inform the choice of your variables and will be the one you discuss in relation to your results in chapter 5. By its nature, a dissertation includes a significant amount of repetition, but only what is necessary. This makes your job easier, but it also means that you need to be sure that you are saying the same thing in each instance. A dissertation chair never wants to read a draft of a proposal and be surprised by a new variable popping up along the way—which means that the writer is sloppy or hasn't taken the time to edit properly.

Separating Your Writing Process from Your Editing Process

In some cases, the writing process is hampered by focusing on getting exactly the *right* words on the page, or by organizing a chapter the *perfect* way. When you are concerned with such issues, you are not writing, you are actually editing. These are very different processes and you need to separate your "writing" self from your "editing" self. Allow yourself to write quite freely and without trying to make things "perfect." This allows you to get all of your thoughts out onto paper or "screen." After you have a very rough draft produced, go back and do your editing—correct spelling, grammar, verb tense agreement, move things around, and put in smooth transitions. You'll be surprised how much progress you can make this way.

Never Wait for Inspiration; Be the Inspiration

Do not be fooled into thinking that people who write a lot are special or magical or that writing can only be done with divine inspiration. Writing is a skill, and like any other skill, it can be learned and it can be honed and improved—this is why the dissertation journal is a good tool. Don't harm your writing—and waste time—by thinking that you need to wait for inspiration to write. In order to write, all that you need to do is *write*. As was discussed previously, don't waste time waiting for conditions to be perfect, they rarely will be.

The Reverse Outline

Using an outline or a reverse outline can be helpful. Most people are familiar with preparing an outline prior to writing an academic paper. In the outline, you create a plan of the points you will discuss in the longer work. This can let you see where you are going with the paper, and provide structure, allow you to see obvious holes in the work as it is developing.

The reverse outline, on the other hand, is developed from a work that is already well underway. You take the written work and create the outline from it. It may seem like this is completely backward, but it allows you to see where the obvious holes are in your writing, including sections that may be overdeveloped. When you create the reverse outline, you can see how many levels of subheadings you are using throughout your entire work. You may need to trim down some areas or beef-up others to create a smooth, balanced product.

Set a Daily (or 5 Days a Week) Schedule and Writing Goal—and Stick to It

Set some sort of schedule for your writing. we would recommend writing five days a week. Some successful dissertation writers have stated that they looked upon the dissertation as a job and spent the hours of 9-5 every weekday working, in some way, on the dissertation. This type of schedule is not realistic for everyone, but the key is they finished the dissertation by making the commitment to do some work on it every day. Set realistic daily writing goals that work with your other regular commitments. Think about how long you can write productively in a single stretch. Perhaps you can write for two hours each day and then you balance the rest of your working time with reading or analyzing data, or even reorganizing and editing. If you write each and every day, you will finish your dissertation. And, if something should happen and you do not stick to your goals—whether it is for a day, or a week, or even months—do not get lost in recriminations: get back to work and reset your goals.

What About the Stuff You Write That You Don't Use?

Finally, don't fall in love with your own writing. Don't get attached to it. Don't identify with it. If you find yourself not wanting to edit material out of a chapter because you spent so much time writing it, keep in mind that the average dissertation writer creates between 3 and 10 times the amount of material that they will actually use in their dissertation. While writing is a big part of the dissertation—editing is a bigger part. The "stuff" that does not wind up in the final product is just a part of the process. When you edit out material, you should save it into a separate document for review later—some of it may be useful as you further edit the dissertation. Some of it may get moved into a different portion of the dissertation. Some of it could serve as ideas for future writing and research that you will do. And some of it will just be deleted—and that's okay.

Topic Cluster: Execution

Execution is the term for the processes used to complete the project. This is the cluster that will take the longest amount of time to progress through, but if you have worked through the previous clusters you will still advance in a timely fashion. In this cluster we will discuss the individual chapters of the dissertation, topic selection, writing and defending your proposal and preparing for the IRB.

Topic: The Chapters of the Dissertation

Your university and/or your department generally will have prescribed the chapters that comprise your dissertation. There may be some leeway to address differences relating to whether you are writing a quantitative or a qualitative dissertation—but dissertations from a single department are fairly similar. This is why you must obtain a copy of the dissertation handbook for your school—look upon this as a starting point in your journey. A common format for the dissertation is five chapters. They are as follows:

- Chapter 1—Introduction
- Chapter 2—Literature review
- Chapter 3—Methods
- Chapter 4—Results
- Chapter 5—Discussion

Even in instances where there are additional chapters, these five are all represented somewhere within the dissertation.

Chapter 1—Introduction

The first chapter presents an introduction to the entire dissertation. It will lead the reader through the entire dissertation in brief format. This chapter introduces your topic, the research variables, and explains in clear terms what is to be gained by conducting this research. While it may be useful to write a sketch of this chapter early on, you will not write the final version of this chapter until the dissertation is complete. If your university has you write a proposal (which will consist of chapters 1, 2, and 3) before beginning your actual data collection, then you will write this chapter after you have finished chapters two and three.

Chapter 2—Literature Review

Chapter 2 presents the literature review. It provides the academic backdrop for your dissertation. Here you will present all of the topical, theoretical, and methodological literature that is relevant to your study (in some situations, the methodological literature will be presented in Chapter 3). You are already used to writing topical literature reviews—as many doctoral level papers are, after all, nothing more than a review of current literature. The topical literature review will focus on literature from the previous decade—i.e., the most current topical literature. You are less accustomed to providing a *theoretical* and *methodological* literature review. The theoretical literature review discusses relevant theories from your discipline and, most specifically, the theory/theories that will provide the underpinning for your study. The theoretical review is *not* confined to works published within the previous 10 years, and should briefly present the historical background of the theory/theories you will be using—generally going all the way back to the founders of the theory/theories. The methodological literature review will discuss both the methodologies and method that have been used to investigate this topic and should also specifically address the methodology and methods that are particular to your study. Again, the methodological literature review does not need to be confined to the past decade and may stretch back for a considerable period of time. It is important to have all three types of literature in your literature review to properly set the stage for your study.

Chapter 3—Methods

Chapter 3 will lay out the methodology for your study. Research is never conducted in a vacuum—everything that you do is based upon the literature and research that has been conducted before it. You will begin by explaining whether you are doing quantitative or a qualitative study. Then you will discuss what type of quantitative or qualitative study you are doing. It is also a good idea to present exactly how your chosen method has been used in your discipline in the past. You will lay out the specific parameters of what you intend to research and identify the research subjects as specifically as you can. Detailed information about your sampling plan, how you will recruit your participants, and how you will collect your data will be included. Be careful that your research proposal does not cross moral or ethical boundaries, but address how any potential ethical issues will be mitigated. You will also describe the analyses that you plan to perform once your data is collected.

Chapter 4—Results

This is the results chapter. It describes the nature of the final sample and will present the data that you have collected and the statistics or the qualitative analysis that you performed. In many quantitative dissertations this is a relatively short chapter, which presents all of the necessary tables/charts/graphs required that display the data and the statistical analyses that were used. In qualitative dissertations, this can be a very lengthy chapter as the analysis of textual data is usually quite complex.

Chapter 5—Discussion

This chapter presents a discussion of the results that were detailed in chapter 4. It is in this chapter that you frame your results in the context of the literature that you presented in chapter 2; you will also provide suggestions for future research that will move the field forward based on your conclusions. Just as you may have found topic ideas in published dissertations that you reviewed, you will complete the circle by providing future doctoral researchers with ideas for potential studies. This chapter may also discuss policy applications or provide suggestions for practical application in the field.

Topic: Selecting a Topic

Without an appropriate topic for your dissertation, there can be no dissertation. The topic is the basis of your work and the foundation upon which everything is built. The stronger the foundation, the less likely you will encounter issues later in the writing process. Just like when building a house, you want to make sure that you have a solid foundation; a solid topic should result in a good dissertation.

If you do not select a topic for your dissertation prior to actually entering the dissertation phase of your doctoral studies, it will considerably lengthen your time in dissertation. If doctoral students have not chosen a topic prior to entering the dissertation phase, they should at least be reading and/or working in one or more areas from which they will choose a topic. This constant reading will allow you to begin building the literature review chapter of your dissertation (chapter 2). If you are still in the reading phase, then you will be able to do very little work on chapter 2—let alone chapters 1 and 3 (the introduction and the methods chapter, respectively).

From "Topic Ideas" to "Topics"

It is useful to differentiate between "topic ideas" and "topics." A "topic idea" is far more vague and general than a "topic." A "topic idea" is a phenomenon in the world that has caught your attention and it may or may not end up being viable to research. There are an infinite number of "topic ideas" out there, but only a limited number of viable "topics" for any field or discipline. Of course, you should begin with "topic ideas," with the goal of fleshing them out into potential topics. Also, please be mindful that while people find topic ideas in a variety of ways, all *topics* ultimately arise from the literature of the discipline.

Some people will enter doctoral studies knowing what topic area they want to conduct their dissertation research in, while for others—myself included—it can seem almost impossible to choose a dissertation topic. This is especially the case if you are generally a curious person and have been very interested in many of the topics that you have encountered during your coursework. It may seem to be an insurmountable task to narrow your focus down to a single topic when there are so many that interest you. We will discuss narrowing down to one topic later.

Common places where topic ideas may arise include: research studies in which you are involved, what you see at work, and the popular media. We have known doctoral students who identified their dissertation topic because they were helping to collect data working on a large research study. In such large studies, there are many data points that aren't being analyzed by the researchers who are conducting the study, and these data points are ripe for analysis by other researchers. Major research institutions often benefit from ample government funding and frequently conduct such studies. We will talk more of the use of secondary data later.

You may observe something in your own work environment that is of interest to you. But be careful—while it may, in fact, be interesting, it may already have been "researched to death" or it may be an issue only of interest to your workplace and not the broader field. Anything that you see in your work environment must be thoroughly examined by going through the current literature. The other hazard of thinking that something at your work could be a good research topic is that your work environment may actually be a dysfunctional environment. The particular problem you see may have been solved a long time ago in the literature, but your workplace may not be implementing best practices.

Another resource for topic ideas is media reports—particularly reporting on current events or social problems. My own topic came from a newspaper article that was in the local paper about gang violence affecting local hospital emergency departments. Again, these topics must also be supported by the broader, academic literature to be viable topics for dissertation.

Although it may seem self-evident, make sure that your topic actually falls within the confines of your discipline. Recently, there has been a push in academia toward more multi-disciplinary and interdisciplinary fields and more general fields; while it is great to be knowledgeable in a variety of areas, don't allow yourself to be pulled away from your discipline—even if you find those outlying areas to be very interesting. For example, a criminal justice student may know very well that school performance can be linked to delinquent behavior; however, to study school performance without that connection to delinquency (or delinquency prevention) effectively takes the criminal justice student outside of his or her discipline. Likewise, the allied health student is certainly aware that many educational institutions are moving away from providing unhealthy snacks to children at school, but to just study schools without the link of "unhealthy snacks" or "unhealthy eating" would be inappropriate.

A word of caution about passion and objectivity in the dissertation process: On the one hand, you want to have a great deal of interest in your topic, yet it's probably not a good idea to choose something that you are too passionate about. You need enough interest and curiosity to carry you through to the end of your dissertation—yet you want to be able to approach your research with objectivity. If you are too passionate about a topic, you might unknowingly engage in research to "prove" something. This is never a good idea since it will blind you to anything that may disprove whatever it is you are trying to prove—in essence, you are far more likely to overlook things or engage in bad science if there is too much passion in what you study. This can be particularly problematic if you are undertaking a qualitative study, as they are often more vulnerable to the effects of researcher bias. You should be very interested in what you are studying, but it should not present any sort of dilemma to you if the results of your research and dissertation come out one way or another.

We have mentioned it before, but it is a point worth reiteration: You should not consider your dissertation and the research contained therein to be your "life's work." You do not want to be working on the dissertation for the remainder of your life. You can use the dissertation as a small piece of what you want your life's work to be—but most importantly; you want to create a study that can be completed in a reasonable amount of time.

To generate a topic, create a list and include the following:

1. General topics in your field that are of interest to you
2. Topics that have interested you in your coursework
3. Topics you researched at the master's level
4. "Suggestions for Future Research" from a variety of dissertations
5. Suggestions from the latest research articles in a number of topic areas
6. Topics that come up frequently in the top five journals in your discipline
7. Work or research that you have been involved in with faculty

General topics in your field that are of interest to you. Creating a list of topics should not be very difficult, as these topics are most likely the reason why you decided to study the discipline that you are in. It's okay to start with some very general or broad topic areas that pique your interest.

Topics that have interested you in your coursework. You might find your topic in one of your courses. Since we can assume that you choose the discipline in which you are pursuing your doctoral degree because it interested you, it is also a good assumption that you will find new topics of interest in the courses that you take. The areas you explore in the shorter papers that you write in courses can be the fodder for the beginning of the literature review for your dissertation, so take the time to explore a variety of areas—especially early on in your coursework.

Topics you researched at the master's level. Your topic might dovetail off of what you did for your master's level research. Major kudos to you if you have experience in conducting research at the master's level, as this can make the dissertation pathway much easier because the dissertation is, after all, research. Doctoral students often lack this preparation.

"Suggestions for Future Research" from a variety of dissertations. Another great way to find a very current topic is to read recent dissertations in your discipline. If you know some general topic areas in which you are interested, you can then find very specific recommendations for your research by reading the "Suggestions for Future Research" in the final chapter of these related dissertations. All dissertations include this (or a similarly titled) section. This is one of the great things about dissertations: unlike regular research articles, dissertations are required to create this bridge to future research. Just as you are now writing your dissertation to prove to the academic world that you possess the research chops to earn the terminal degree, many, many others have written dissertations before you. One of the key requirements for a dissertation is that it is new and different research, and in turn, each dissertation will also provide suggestions for continuing and building on this new research. That makes this an excellent first place to start looking, but be aware that all dissertations are *not* created equal. Not just any dissertation will provide you with great ideas for your research—you may need to review more than a handful to come up with a viable topic that interests you, but it is something to consider.

Suggestions from the latest research articles in a number of topic areas. Read current journal articles to identify topics. Journals have the benefit of exposing you to what is both cutting-edge and what is considered to be very important in your field. Many journal articles will also include a section at the end where the authors will discuss what they would do differently if they were to conduct the study again, or will—like all dissertations—provide suggestions for follow-up research.

Topics that come up frequently in the top five journals in your discipline. You should be reading as much as you possibly can during your doctoral studies. It is important for you to identify the top journals in your field very early on. Pay attention to the topics that seem to come up frequently in them. These are the really "hot" topics in your field. While there are probably a lot of articles written on these topics, it should be easy for you to find good gaps in the literature to research. Another benefit of conducting research in one of these "hot" areas is that you may even be able to obtain funding for your dissertation.

Work or research that you have been involved in with faculty. You might identify your topic by working directly with a faculty member who is conducting research in a particular area that interests you; this is a great way to find something to do for your dissertation. Because you will be advancing the research of the faculty member with whom you are working, he or she will have quite an interest in what you are doing. This can be a great help to you—although be careful about bias: that faculty member may have a very vested interest in the outcome of your research—and this can be either a help or a hindrance to your work. This can also lead to having your name on publications and provide you with very obvious dissertation topics. However, since you are paid very little for this work and the faculty member can derive great benefit from having you around—they may want you to stay for a long time and not be anxious to see you finish your work in just twelve or 18-

months. You may also need to consider what might happen if your research conclusions contradict that faculty member's research. While a good and worthwhile faculty member and researcher should welcome this sort of challenge, academia—like many institutions—is filled with petty individuals who might see fit instead to discredit you, or even vigorously endeavor to prevent you from finishing your degree. We still stand by the assertion that "piggy-backing" onto existing research in which you may already be involved is a very viable way of developing your dissertation—you just need to be aware upfront of the personalities involved and the conflicts that could potentially arise. It is better to think of this before investing the time, then to find yourself mired in that rare, delicate situation afterward. This option does not necessitate that you conduct your own research based upon that faculty member's research; you could consider using that faculty member's data for secondary data analysis—more on this option later.

Topic: Broad Topic to Specific Topic

Even after you have selected a topic, it needs to be made sufficiently narrow and specific to research it effectively. A topic that is too broad is almost as bad as having no topic at all. We have seen many students fall into this trap and really struggle to get a handle on their topic. Having too broad of a topic can lead to endless strands of literature. It will pose difficulties for selection of variables—easily leading to having too many research variables or variables that are too vague or provide inconclusive data.

If you are thinking on the level of "social problems," then your topic is too broad. You may be interested in "correlates of delinquency," but the causes of delinquency are too broad a topic for a dissertation—remember that a dissertation is really only a single book, and there are hundreds of books devoted to correlates of delinquency, along with a myriad of journal articles. The challenge here is two-fold:

First you need to narrow down the topic, perhaps by focusing on a particular population, such as "correlates of delinquency among indigenous peoples of Canada." Even that, however, is still too broad—you must make it even more specific to make it easily researchable. The next step would be: "correlates of delinquency among 13-16 year-old Inuit females in Northern British Columbia." Your topic is now sufficiently narrow, and your research subjects are identified and quantifiable in such a way that we can obtain a representative sample for conducting research.

Secondly, you now need to go back to the literature—remember, you should have been reading the literature from your first thoughts about topic and since the beginning of your doctoral studies—to make sure that you have, indeed, found a gap *that warrants researching*. If this isn't a gap, perhaps looking at "risk and protective factors" is better, or "programming aimed at lowering rates of delinquency" among 13–16 year-old Inuit females in Northern British Columbia. The only way to ensure you have found a gap is to perform an exhaustive literature review of your topic area.

It can be difficult to determine what actually warrants researching: in the final analysis, it is up to the discipline. The existing literature in your field is the most important indicator of whether or not a topic should be pursued. If you are finding articles related to or addressing your topic in the top journals in your discipline, then that is usually a good sign. If no literature exists on your topic, there are two possibilities (1) you have identified a gap in the literature, (2) your discipline is not interested in your topic and/or it cannot be readily studied. Only a thorough reading of the existing research will help you determine what situation you are in with your topic.

It is equally important to eliminate topics from your list as it is to add them. It might prove very difficult to find an appropriate gap in the literature for topics that have received a lot of research attention. A topic such as "alcoholism" is both very broad and very well researched. If you go to an academic database and type in "alcoholism" as a search term you will get thousands of hits; if you search for books on "alcoholism" you will come upon thousands of books. There is so much to read to just get the background on alcoholism that it can be insurmountable—where would you start? Where is the gap? On the other hand, if you have been working in the area of addictions for a number of years and have been involved in other research in the area of alcoholism, you might be perfectly prepared to find the gap in the literature that merits review and to conduct research in this area. However, if you are not already well acquainted with this topic area, and if you aren't prepared to read all of the necessary background literature, then this is clearly a topic that should be eliminated—even if you have a keen interest in addictions. It is important to note again that working in the area in which you are doing your research—or having worked in the area—may also serve to blind you to the actual results of your study.

Topic: Quickly Choosing a Topic

It may be necessary in some cases to choose a topic quickly and to review the literature in a similar expedient manner. Perhaps you are already in the dissertation phase of your studies and maybe you are running out of funding. Or perhaps you were previously pursuing a different topic but that is no longer a possibility. In such a situation, what do you do?

- Choose a topic that has secondary data available with a very clear research gap—perhaps a gap suggested by the creators of the data
- Once you make a choice, stick with it; remember there are plenty of interesting topics in your discipline but you can only research one for your dissertation—the important thing it to just make a choice
- Ask a faculty member whom you respect—or who has a research area in which you have some interest—to make a suggestion
- Use the UMI Dissertation Abstracts database and pull 50 recent dissertations in your discipline:
  - Make a list of topics that appear frequently
  - Make a list of topics that interest you
  - Read their "Suggestions for Future Research" and see what strikes you
- If there is not a single clear topic that interests you, make a list of three of the most interesting topics in your field, then spend several days exploring each topic in greater detail and select the one that:
  - Interests you the most
  - Seems most feasible
  - Has the most obvious research gap

Topic: Writing the Literature Review

Timeline Reminder

Upon reviewing the sample timeline you created in the Planning Cluster of this book, you will see that the recommendation was that you have a draft of the literature review completed prior to entering the dissertation phase of your doctoral studies. This means that you will be constantly working on the literature review during your time in coursework: writing and rewriting and discarding and editing all the while. When you enter dissertation, it should be your goal to spend one solid month polishing the literature review for your dissertation. You will polish this chapter first since it serves as the backdrop for your entire study.

If you were unable to work on the literature review prior to actually entering dissertation, do not despair. The literature review will take you longer than a month, but there are definite tips that you can employ to complete the literature review as quickly as possible. You will find these tips at the end of this topic.

Tools Reminder

We also discussed a number of tools in the Planning Cluster that will be very useful to you in creating your literature review and you may want to revisit them now. Of particular interest is the research log, which can help you organize and track the information that you discover upon reading the many books and articles you will include in your literature review. It may be beneficial to utilize an outline or a reverse outline during the writing process. Finally, make good use of the many tools available to you from your library—as mentioned in the "Research Tips and Tricks" section. Some of my favorites include "cited reference searching," and "author and journal notifications."

What is the Literature Review?

The literature review is Chapter 2 of the dissertation, and is most likely the chapter that you will be working on first, since it provides the academic backdrop for why your study is important and why it should be conducted. It may also be the easiest of the dissertation chapters that you write because it looks very much like the majority of papers that you have written during your academic career. Even at the undergraduate level, most papers that you wrote were simply reviews of the literature on a particular topic. That is what you are doing now, except on a grander scale.

If you are going to write an twelve or18-month dissertation, you will not begin the literature review the day you enter the dissertation phase of your doctoral studies, but you should instead have been writing the literature review from very early on in your doctoral career. Students who are very good at planning will begin to write pieces of the literature review in each and every class they take—some will even begin exploring possible dissertation topics during their master or bachelor's level studies. While it is not necessary that you begin writing the literature review that early—or even at the beginning of your doctoral studies—you should certainly be writing some of your papers and building some of your literature review during your coursework. At the very least, you should use coursework to explore potential topics. The more you can read and compile ahead of time, the shorter your eventual time will be in dissertation. If you have not chosen a topic at the outset of your coursework, begin to review the relevant literature in several areas and explore them in different courses.

The Three Types of Literature Reviews

There are basically three types of literature reviews that you will need to include in your dissertation: topical, theoretical, and methodological. In some cases, the methodological literature review is found only in chapter 3 of the dissertation; at other times, you will find it addressed briefly in chapter 2 and more fully in chapter 3 methods. Consult your school's dissertation manual (or other dissertations from your department) and seek advice from your chair as per specific guidelines on the structure of your own dissertation.

The typical literature review presents the information needed to provide a backdrop for the readers of your study. It should not be so broad that it goes on for 100+ pages, but long enough to allow the average student in your discipline to understand the framework of the study. Keep in mind that the purpose of the dissertation is to represent an advance in the literature in your discipline, and that your dissertation will, in turn, be used by other students in the discipline (and not just academicians who have been researching in the field for many years) so write with the student-audience in mind. Keep in mind that although you are familiar with the language of your field, your readers may not be and define any terms that the layperson may find unfamiliar. It may present a brief history of the topic, a good discussion of the variables (concepts), and perhaps some of the main debates in the subject area. The literature review is often the longest chapter of the dissertation and should be as long as is necessary to provide the background for your study, but literature reviews typically average from 25-50 pages in length in most dissertations.

The topical review. Writing the *topical* literature review should be the least difficult portion of the literature review to write. Most graduate papers are really literature reviews. The topical literature review will cover the important aspects of the topic that your reader will need to understand to appreciate your study. It may present a brief history of how the research on that topic has developed. During the topical literature review you will present the background on the variables that you have chosen (and have not chosen) for your study. Depending upon how much research exists, this can be quite lengthy. You may also need to discuss literature on your topic that appears outside of your discipline.

The theoretical literature review. A theory is a set of interrelated statements that explain a phenomenon. For the dissertation, theory represents the underpinning of your study. It will inform and impact your choice of variables, how you analyze your data, and how you write up your data. For example, if social learning theory provides the theoretical underpinning of your dissertation, then "learning" will be important to your dissertation. Conversely, if cognitive dissonance theory is the underpinning, your dissertation must deal with a situation in which individuals have two or more cognitions that clash. You can imagine how two dissertations on an identical topic employing these two varied theories, would yield very different final products. If you want to quickly glance at some of the wide variety of theories that have been created in different disciplines, go to *www.changingminds.org.* You will find that a theory has been created for just about everything!

Writing the *theoretical* literature review is often more difficult than the topical literature review. Many graduate programs touch very little upon theory, so graduate students often lack a firm understanding of theory—even if they have had theory-based classes. Many theory courses, unfortunately, do not provide strong tie-ins to the research of the discipline.

There are several good ways to become acquainted with the theories in your discipline, so do not despair or feel you need to do a lot of catch-up work to write the theoretical portion of your literature review. The easiest way to become immersed in theory is to read a good general theory text—and if you have not already done this for your discipline, you should do so anyway. This will provide you with the context of how theory is used in your discipline, and likely give a brief historical overview of theory as well. While this is a good starting place, it is not enough to simply choose a theory from your discipline; the chosen theory must also be *appropriate for your topic*, for the variables you've chosen, and for your analysis. Return to all of those articles and dissertations you used for your topical literature review and examine them for theories (hopefully, you can consult your research log and identify the different theories that have been used to address your topic). Some articles provide theoretical discussions and most dissertations do. You may also conduct theoretical searches through databases by using appropriate search terms for your topic, and search terms such as "theory," or the names of particular theories. It is important to note that your references for theory may be considerably older than most of the references you use for your dissertation. Often theories are decades old. This is okay. It is also important to note developments in the theory over time in addition to the original source.

If you find yourself in the situation where the theories that are coming up in the dissertations and articles that you have read do not provide the underpinning you desire for your study, you may need to look at theories in other disciplines. This can be particularly viable if your dissertation is bridging together two or more disciplines or if you are in a newly developing field.

The methodological literature review. The methodological literature review can be found either in chapter 2 or chapter 3. Some departments prefer to save it for chapter 3, which addresses method within the dissertation. Even if your methodological literature review will appear in chapter 3, you should still provide a brief sketch of it in chapter 2 as a means of orienting your reader.

In the methodological literature review you will provide a general background for the methodology you have chosen—qualitative or quantitative—but not so much that it seems you are writing a method text. This should be looked at as a general orientation to what you are doing. Be mindful that you are not teaching someone about qualitative or quantitative methodology. You are expected to discuss the particular quantitative or qualitative approach you will be employing, for example, case study or non-experimental survey research. Then you will follow this up by presenting some of the literature within your discipline (and topic) that utilizes the same approach you are using.

Choosing your methodological approach should not be difficult. There is no need to reinvent the wheel when it comes to methodology. When you design your study, it can save you time and effort if you model it after other studies that have been conducted in your discipline. Your variables will, of course, be different, but the methodological structure is the same. Stick with what you have seen in the literature in your discipline and design a similar study. This will help your study fit comfortably in with previous studies that have been conducted in the discipline.

This is also a good time to pay attention to whether or not your discipline favors certain types of studies—and conducts many of them. Some disciplines are more open to qualitative approaches than others. Different disciplines even favor the use of certain statistics over others. Again, use your research log and see what methodologies you have come across in your reading. If you feel that you must use a methodological approach or statistics that you have not come across in the literature in your discipline, remember that you will be tasked with providing a justification for your choice. This might be perfectly okay, and it may be the case that this aspect of your study is new and different. By utilizing a different methodological approach than one that is regularly employed in your discipline, new conclusions may come to light.

General Tips for the Literature Review

Like any type of writing, writing the literature review takes a lot of practice. There are some general tips that you should keep in mind to make the writing of a literature review easier:

- Read plenty of literature reviews and mimic the styles you like—or the styles that are widely accepted in your discipline
- Write the literature review in the format suggested here: topical, theoretical, and methodological
- Remember your literature review needs to provide a background for your study; approach it as if you had never read about your study before—what would someone need to know
- Everything that is a part of your study should be covered in some way in the literature review—new variables or constructs should not appear in chapter 3 that have not been addressed in chapter 2
- Don't try to provide an exhaustive literature review of everything that has ever been done that is related to your study—remember that appropriate focus is important too—concentrate on the peer-reviewed literature from the past 5-10 years and synthesize and integrate these findings in your chapter
- Since you must read a lot before you write your literature review, it is very important to keep the notes on what you have read well-organized
- Be certain to keep all of the information handy that you will need to properly cite each item; consider utilizing a reference management program

Starting the Literature Review Late

Not everyone begins the literature review for their dissertation when they start doctoral studies. I (O'Reilly) didn't begin my dissertation literature review until two semesters before I finished coursework. It is not the worst thing in the world to start the literature review later rather than sooner.

When you begin your literature review, remember that everything relating to your proposed study—and helps sets the backdrop for it—is a part of it. Go back to related papers that you have written and mine your references for re-use. Go through bibliographies you have written; review your own journal and author alerts—all of these resources will provide you with potential material for your literature review. Even if you have selected your dissertation topic very late, it is unlikely that you will be starting totally from "square one." Keep in mind that all the work you've done during your doctoral studies—everything you've read is in your head and it is informing the choices that you make in your study. You most likely will have at least touched upon your topic in some peripheral way, and you will have read about many theories during the course of your doctoral studies and learned a great deal about methodology. All of this will provide material for your literature review.

Topic: Writing Chapter 3—Methodology and Method

Timeline Reminder

Upon review of the sample timeline that you created in the Planning Cluster of this book, you will see that the recommendation was for that you have a draft of Chapter 3—your methodology chapter—completed prior to entering the dissertation phase of your doctoral studies. In order to accomplish this, you need to be working on this chapter while you are still doing your coursework—ideally in conjunction with your writing of Chapter 2. You will then spend one month polishing this chapter with the assistance of your Chair once you are formally in dissertation.

Tools Reminder

We discussed the research log and the dissertation journal in the "Research Tips and Tricks" section of the Planning Cluster. Both the log and journal will be very useful to you in the creation of your methodology chapter. By consulting the research log, you will be able to track each and every journal article you read. This will also give you a quick way to see what methodologies and methods other researchers have employed to conduct studies in your discipline—which, in turn, should inform the choices you make for Chapter 3.

What is the Methodology?

The methodology (sometimes also called methods) chapter explains, in great detail, how your study will be conducted—with emphasis on "great detail." It should be viewed like a recipe for your study and must be specific enough that anyone could read the recipe, follow it, and know *exactly* how to replicate your study.

What is presented here is a general outline for what is contained in a methodology chapter. Keep in mind that your university and department may discuss some of these steps differently and you may find different terminology used in some of the methodological literature.

The methodology chapter should cover, at a minimum, the following:

- The methodology
- The design
- The research questions
- The variables or concepts
- The methods used to collect data
- The identification of the subjects
- The steps you will take to recruit your subjects
- How the data will be collected
- How the data will be analyzed
- Ethical considerations

You will also write an introduction and a conclusion. Like all introductions and conclusions, these sections tell the reader what you will be telling them, and, later reiterate what you told them. Once the other pieces are written, the introduction and conclusion are easy to craft and write—so leave them until last.

Methodology. You have three basic choices for your methodology: quantitative, qualitative, and mixed. Quantitative deals primarily with numbers as data and you will analyze your data through the use of particular statistics. Qualitative deals primarily with words and you will use a variety of techniques to analyze mostly word data. A mixed-methods study is really more like two studies that are conducted in conjunction with each other, one of which is quantitative and one of which is qualitative. Don't be confused by the term "mixed-methods." It does not mean that you just mix together the things you do in quantitative and the things you do in qualitative in any manner, and that becomes your study. "Mixed-methods," instead, is a very complex approach that almost requires what would amount to two separate studies. We would recommend a mixed-methods approach only when the research questions and the study absolutely call for it—otherwise, stick to doing either quantitative or qualitative.

Several things determine the methodology you choose for your dissertation: your discipline, your research questions, and how quickly you plan to complete the dissertation. In my experience working with students at the dissertation stage, quantitative dissertations are easier to finish than qualitative ones. This may seem counter-intuitive, since many people seem to have a fear of math and statistics—and that is what quantitative deals with—while qualitative deals primarily with words as data. But, as it turns out, it is far easier to learn some basic statistics and crunch the numbers than it is to learn how to deal with the interpretation of data derived from long interviews, for example.

From my experience, if you want to do a qualitative dissertation, you need to be willing to put in more time (and money), and must make the commitment to doing it right—my (O'Reilly) own dissertation employed a qualitative methodology—and I learned valuable lessons from the experience that have affected both how I teach and approach research—but it did take me five years to complete the dissertation.

A word of caution: do not choose to conduct a qualitative study just because you do not want to do the statistical analysis necessary for a quantitative dissertation. Anyone who earns a Ph.D. in a social science *should* know how to conduct a quantitative study and should know how to use statistics—if for no other reason than you need to be able to read and understand the literature in your field. Also keep in mind that while qualitative has gained considerable respect over the past thirty years, most social science disciplines rely upon and expect studies to be quantitative in nature—and funding is generally driven by quantitative studies.

Design. The design of your study is the succinct explanation of how your data will be collected and analyzed. Within the broad methodologies of quantitative and qualitative, there are a variety of designs that can be used. There are also mixed methods designs in which part of the study is conducted qualitatively and part of the study is quantitative. As noted previously, these tend to be more complex because you must collect and analyze both qualitative and quantitative data. Details of a variety of the design options follow.

Quantitative design. In quantitative research there are four basic designs: descriptive, correlational, causal-comparative/quasi-experimental research, and experimental research. Let's take a moment to discuss each of these.

Descriptive. In a descriptive study, you are merely describing what is in the world. This is very basic research and generally at the dissertation level in quantitative, descriptive research is not enough. Descriptive research can tell us about rates (for example, recidivism rates), or means (for example, the mean math score for high school seniors on their state graduation test). While these things will likely be reported in your dissertation, generally departments want you to go beyond these simple statistics for your study.

Correlational. Correlational studies describe the relationship between and among variables. There is no manipulation of variables, no control over variables is exercised, and there is no random assignment to groups. A correlational study might look at how client satisfaction relates to growth within a particular industry. Note that some people consider correlational studies to also be descriptive research.

Causal-comparative/quasi-experimental. These studies are similar to experiments, but two of the key elements required for a true experiment are missing: first, there is no random assignment to groups (the researcher must use groups that already exist); and second, in causal-comparative, the researcher does not manipulate the independent variable. While the effects of the independent variable on the dependent variable are measured and analyzed, you must be very careful when making statements about causation in this type of a study because many different factors could be influencing the independent variable. Ensuring that the groups are similar in other respects can minimize this limitation somewhat.

Experimental. This approach is often referred to as a "true experiment." There must be random assignment of subjects to groups in an experiment, and the researcher will manipulate the independent variables and also try to exercise control over the variables; this allows statements about cause and effect to be made. In the social sciences, true experiments are uncommon because of how difficult it can be to meet the criteria of random assignment, manipulation of variables, and control of variables. In many instances, what we wish to investigate cannot ethically be investigated through a true experiment; for example, can you imagine assigning children randomly to groups of "abuse" and "non-abuse?" So, causal-comparative studies are often more practical in the social sciences.

Qualitative design. It can be difficult to create a definitive list of qualitative designs since a case could be made that some of the designs that we discuss here overlap or might more correctly be considered a philosophical approach to research rather than just a design. For our purposes, however, the qualitative designs are: case study, phenomenology, ethnography, grounded theory, and narrative.

Case study. The case study is the most commonly utilized qualitative design. It looks at a "bounded system," or a case. There are a variety of different types of case studies—ones that employ only qualitative methods—you may even come across quantitative case studies in the literature. Many case studies allow for the use of both quantitative and qualitative methods. Although case studies may be comprised of only a single person, it is more common to be studying a group that is bounded by a work or school environment. Case studies of a single individual are often not approved for dissertation research, as their transferability is so limited. Another key component of the case study is the triangulation of data, which means that multiple types of data are collected to create a more complete picture of what is being studied. My own dissertation was a case study that examined perceptions of violence in the emergency department.

Phenomenology. The phenomenological study seeks to get at the research participant's "lived experience" of some phenomenon. The goal of this research is to detail for the reader essentially what it is like to be that person in that experience. These studies are often very moving—allowing the reader a glimpse into the lives of the participants.

Ethnography. Originating from anthropology, ethnography looks at cultures, subcultures, or micro-cultures. The research will necessarily be involved in looking at language, rituals, beliefs, values, practices, and norms. The research will have as its goal to describe the culture, subculture or micro-culture and how these ideals held by this group affect their daily lives.

Grounded theory. In grounded theory the researcher creates theory from the "ground up." It is expected that the data will lead the researcher to create new theory. This can be a very challenging approach for students, as it requires a thorough grasp of existing theory that many students are lacking.

Narrative. This approach employs the stories (narratives) of people to explain what you are interested in. It can focus either on the individual or on a group. Common methods in this approach include field notes, journals, letters, photos, family stories, oral history and autobiographies. This approach can also be used with online artifacts like blogs, emails and texts. In all cases, the researcher will extract meaning from the text of the narratives. There are a variety of types of narrative analyses and focuses within narrative analysis.

Mixed methods design. Mixed-methods design can be defined in various ways. The research in some instances of mixed-methods design consists of conducting a quantitative portion of the study followed in turn by a qualitative portion of the study (or vice-versa); this is sometimes referred to as a "sequential mixed-methods design." There is also a mixed methods design in which the quantitative and qualitative portions of the study are conducted simultaneously—which is referred to as "concurrent mixed-methods design." You will find a variety of other mixed designs in the literature. These studies are usually more difficult to conduct because they require that you be very good at both quantitative and qualitative research. If you are interested in mixed-methods, be sure to read the methodological literature closely and choose a chair who is comfortable with mixed-methods. It is beyond the scope of this text to provide an in-depth discussion of this complex methodology.

The research questions. The research questions are the broad over-arching questions that will be answered by the dissertation. For example: "What are the lived experiences of economically disadvantaged Hurricane Katrina survivors?" or "How do high school GPA, SAT scores and gender relate to completion of an undergraduate degree?" These should not be confused with "interview questions," which are the specific questions that you would be asking your participants if you are conducting interviews in your research.

It might seem overly simplistic to state this, but research questions must be written as questions—with a question mark. If they are written as statements, they are more like hypotheses, which are statements about what you expect to happen in your research.

The research questions should clearly name all of the variables in the study—although control variables will not be named. Any research question that lists two or more variables must be quantitative, while qualitative research questions will have only one general concept.

Research questions often hint at the methodological approach used in the study. Research questions that use words such as "predict," "relate," and "effect" are quantitative, while research questions that use words such as "lived experiences," "explore," or "discover," are qualitative.

Quantitative research will include both hypotheses and null hypotheses. Hypotheses—as stated previously—are statements of what the researcher expects the results of the research to be. These are very much like the research questions, except they are written in the form of a statement, for example: "SAT scores will relate to completion of an undergraduate degree." The null hypotheses are simply the opposite of the hypotheses—that there will be no relation between the variables. For example, "There will be no relationship between SAT scores and completion of an undergraduate degree." Hypotheses are guided by what has been found in the previous literature on your topic.

Variables. The variables in a quantitative study or the concepts in a qualitative study are what the researcher is interested in examining. They are the "objects" of the study. In a quantitative study the variables must be clearly defined (often referred to as "operationally defined") and measureable. A variable might be "job satisfaction," "depression," or "gender."

In qualitative studies, the researcher investigates a concept or concepts. These are more nebulous than quantitative variables. A concept in a qualitative study might be "the lived experience of Hurricane Katrina survivors" or "the experiences of grandparents raising grandchildren."

Methods used to collect data. The "methods" that you use in your dissertation are the ways in which you collect your data. There are both quantitative and qualitative methods.

Quantitative methods. Common quantitative data collections methods include structured interviews, quantitative coded observations, surveys, instruments, and physiologic measures.

Measurement. One of the most important parts of a quantitative study is choosing reliable and valid instruments to measure your variables of interest. In order to determine the reliability and validity of an instrument, psychometric evaluations are conducted. This ensures that the instrument is actually measuring what it purports to measure and that it does so consistently. This is a fairly involved process and is generally beyond the scope of a dissertation (unless that is your sole focus). For this reason, you do not want to make up your own instruments. For your dissertation, you want to choose instruments that have already been developed and tested. Your analyses are only as strong as your measurement tools. For example, the Beck Depression Inventory is a 21-item instrument to assess depression with clinical cut-offs. It has been determined to be reliable and valid and has been normed on literally thousands of individuals. Compare that to a one-item measure: How depressed are you on a scale of 1-10? This would be a very weak, and not psychometrically sound way of measurement. The BDI would be a much better choice. Choose your instruments carefully. Measurement tools can be found in the Mental Measurements Yearbook database in your school's library, in peer-reviewed articles that you read, and in dissertations. Be sure to report the psychometric data for your instrument when describing it in your dissertation.

Qualitative methods. Common qualitative data collection methods include semi-structured or unstructured interviews, field notes, and qualitative observations. There are also other, less frequently used, qualitative data-collection methods, including have subjects draw pictures or take photographs.

The qualitative interview. In dissertations, perhaps the most common method for qualitative data collection is the qualitative interview. A qualitative interview should be either semi-structured or unstructured. The semi-structured interview will utilize guiding interview questions. The unstructured interview, a much more complex type of interview, does not utilize an interview guide but allows the subject to speak with very little guidance by the researcher. The unstructured interview is more commonly used when conducting life history interviews—as opposed to interviews during a case study.

Semi-structured interviews provide a guideline for what questions should be asked during the interview process, but also provide flexibility so that the interviewer can explore interesting topics as each interviewee reveals them. The questions in the interview guide do not need to be asked in any particular order, but in whatever order works best for each subject.

Field notes. Field notes can be used in at least two different ways in qualitative research. They can be used as a self-check by the researcher or they can be used as a method of data collection. Field notes should be kept in all qualitative research as a method of self-check by the researcher. Within the field notes the researcher can record observations, can explore biases, or even make notes for use during the data analysis phase. Field notes can also serve as a method of data collection. When this is done, a specific plan for analysis must be created.

Qualitative observations. Qualitative observations are very different from their quantitative counterpart. While quantitative observations rely upon very structured counting of clearly operationalized events, qualitative observation strives to capture the more general "feel" of what is being observed.

Variables. The variables (sometimes referred to as "concepts" in qualitative) are those things that are being measured in your study. Do not confuse them with "population descriptors," which merely describe the population upon which you are focusing in your study. Consider the following research question: "How do undergraduate GPA, marital status, and presence of children in the household relate to the stress level of female graduate students in a healthcare administration graduate program?" The independent variables in the study are "undergraduate GPA," "marital status," and "presence of children in the household." The dependent variable is "stress level." But "female" is just a population descriptor as gender is not a variable in this study. All of the subjects are women and, as the name implies, a variable must *vary*—so we know that "female" cannot be a variable in this study.

Variables in a quantitative study must be measureable and quantifiable. As far as the "measurement" of a variable is concerned, two important questions must be answered: "What is the *level* of measurement?" and "How will the variable be measured?"

There are four levels of measurement: nominal, ordinal, interval and ratio. In the social sciences, these four levels of measurement are usually collapsed into two: "categorical" (which is nominal) and non-categorical (which are any of the other three); the social sciences are usually not dealing with variables that are interval or ratio. A *nominal variable* is one in which the classifications are merely names or labels. These variables are typically groups. Gender is a nominal variable, as is political party; being male or female does not imply better, or more or less of anything—they are merely names of categories. An *ordinal variable* is a variable that implies some sort of order—as the name implies. For example, first-born, second-born, third-born. When we use these levels, we know that in any family the first-born is older than the second-born, but we do not know how many months or years (or minutes in the case of twins!) are between them. Likert-type scales, where participants are asked to rate a response on a scale of 1-7, are also ordinal scales. Most tools to measure constructs in the social sciences provide this type of data. When employing an *interval variable* the distance between any two intervals should be the same. Income, when recorded as a number (not a range) in an interval variable. We know that the person who makes $50,000 makes twice as much as the person who makes $25,000. A *ratio variable* must have a meaningful "zero point" beyond which nothing being studied can exist. Most measurement in the physical sciences is conducted using ratio scales such as mass, length and duration.

All of the variables in your study must be measured in some way. Categorical variables—like gender or political affiliation—can be measured by having the subjects identify to which category they belong—and it is up to you, as the researcher, to make sure than you provide appropriate categories that will account for everyone in your study. For the variable "gender" the choices are fairly obvious—male or female—unless you are conducting a study that will include special populations in it: for example, dealing with gender identity. In that case you will need to give more thought to what the choices should be for the subjects. Perhaps this can be addressed by two questions instead of one: "What is your birth gender?" and "What is your gender identification?" If "political affiliation" is the variable, you will need to decide what categories should be used in your study. It may be the case that "Democrat" and "Republican" will be enough, but you may need to provide other options such as "Independent," "Unaffiliated," or "Other." The decisions that you make regarding what sort of options to allow your subjects to choose from will have definite bearing on your study. It can cause serious problems for your data collection and analysis if you have subjects who feel that none of the categories apply to them, they may decide not to answer at all or skip various questions and then you will have missing data.

You will need to make choices about how you will measure your variables. For example, we commonly see age measured by having subjects choose an age range to which they belong, such as 18-24. Anyone who has participated in market research has seen this. This transforms the variable "age" from interval data into nominal (or categorical) data—which is the least robust type of data and will allow only for certain statistical analysis. But age can also be measured as a number, such as "24" or "37;" this is what is referred to as "score data"—data that comes from interval or ratio levels of measurement (in this case interval). It is also non-categorical data and can provide you with a lot of information and allow you to do more complex statistical analyses. As a general rule, it is always better to collect score data (if it is possible). Collect "age" as a number, then if you want (or need) to collapse the data into ranges (categories), you can do that—but you cannot do the reverse and expand data that has been collected as a range into the actual ages of the subjects.

Score data is ideal for conducting powerful statistical analyses. Many commonly used measures produce score data, such as IQ tests and psychological measures of depression or anxiety. Even educational tests for math or reading generally produce score data. Almost any measure in which you end up with a number as a result is score data.

Quantitative studies will have both independent and dependent variables, and you may also have control variables. The independent variable is the variable(s) that you believe has/have an impact or influence on the dependent variable. Control variables are variables that are kept constant during the research because they could impact the study or skew the results—so we control for them. If you were interested in whether or not seventh graders got higher test scores under certain lighting conditions you would want to hold other important factors constant so that they do not influence test scores—such as time of day the tests were administered, type of tests that were administered and so forth. Whether a variable is treated as an independent or dependent variable in your analyses is guided by your understanding of the variables based on your reading of the literature. Some variables must be treated as independent variables because of temporal precedence—they predate the dependent variable. For example, when examining the relation between behavior problems in elementary school and juvenile delinquency problems in high school, behavior problems in elementary school must be the independent variable. However, if you are interested in the relation between associating with delinquent peers and engaging in delinquent behaviors the choice of which is independent and which is dependent may be less clear and must be guided by your understanding of the literature.

The number of independent and dependent variables that you have in your study will impact the statistic that you choose for your study. If you were looking at how two variables relate to each other, then you would perform a correlation. If you were looking at how more than two variables relate to each other, then you would perform a regression. If you were looking at a difference between two groups, then you would perform a t-test. If you were looking at a difference among three or more groups, then you would perform an Analysis of Variance. Of course, there is much more involved in choosing an appropriate statistic for your research and a full discussion is beyond the scope of this text, but you should be aware of the importance of understanding the nature of your variables.

The measurement of a variable in qualitative is not as clear-cut as it is in quantitative research. Variables in qualitative are generally referred to as concepts and may be broader in scope. Qualitative variables are often measured through the analysis of long interviews or come from the analysis of some form of word-data—such as diaries or newspaper clippings.

The researcher will often try to derive "themes" from the data. All qualitative variables are considered to be categorical variables.

Identification of the subjects. The subjects in the study are the individuals who take part in your research. They may also be referred to as "participants." In qualitative, they will sometimes be referred to as "co-researchers"—this can be confusing, but by using this term, qualitative researchers are acknowledging the importance of the individuals from whom they collect data.

Most types of quantitative and qualitative research require the use of subjects—although qualitative research utilizes fewer subjects than quantitative. Studies involving the use of secondary data are one of the exceptions: in a secondary data analysis, you will not need to recruit subjects because data has already been collected—either for a previous study, or by an agency or organization in the course of doing business. We will discuss secondary data later.

Who should be in the study? In many cases, a research study will require certain specific categories of subjects. If you are researching leadership styles in non-profit organizations, you will need subjects who have leadership roles in non-profits or the employees of these leaders. If you are interested in nurses' perceptions of violence in the emergency department, then you will need to recruit nurses. Your dissertation must describe exactly who your subjects are—this might include their gender, age range, where they live, and the type of profession in which they are employed—depending upon your study. For example, your research may require a group comprised of "delinquent girls ages 14-18 in a large, urban area," or your subjects may be "adult heart patients over the age of 55."

Subjects are often recruited because they are convenient. A lot of research has been done using undergraduate psychology students as subjects; while this research does tell us something it may not be generalizable to other populations. You need to choose your subjects carefully or you might come up with unusual results or may even end up measuring something you didn't intend to measure. If you were conducting a study about sexual attitudes of adult females over the age of 35, but you recruited from a church population, then the responses that you receive on your survey may not be generalizable to all women over the age of 35. In this case, you might actually be introducing a confounding variable into the study—being involved in an organized religion. Depending upon what denomination the church was, the impact on the study could be considerable, as some religious denominations have very socially conservative members: if your study is not aimed at looking at sexual attitudes of adult female members of that particular religious group, then you had better choose subjects from another population!

You need to be very clear on what type of subject your study calls for. Examine the list of categories below and consider what population descriptors matter for your study.

- Gender
- Age
- Race or ethnicity
- Geographic location
- Profession or position
- Political affiliation
- Religious affiliation
- Education
- Diagnosis, disease, or disability

These are just a few of the many population descriptors that might be important for your study, and there are many, many more. The population descriptors, which are important for your study, will be directly related to the variables that you have chosen to investigate. You also need to be careful that if you choose to target a population descriptor or variable that you will be able to find those subjects. In some studies, it might make sense to include individuals of different religious backgrounds, in others, it might not matter.

Subject recruitment. You will also need to consider where you will find the subjects who will participate in your research, and how you can ethically include them in your study. There are guidelines to which you must adhere when selecting subjects; some of these guidelines are based on ethical concerns—which we will discuss later in the cluster on preparing for the Institutional Review Board.

There are some people that you generally cannot recruit to be in your research study. You should not already know or have a professional relationship with your subjects. If you have friends participate in your research, they may try to please you with their responses—which will bias your research. You should avoid dual relationships with your subjects: a doctor would not recruit his or her own patients—neither would a therapist. In both of these cases, the subjects might want to please the researcher, introducing bias into the study—or even feel that they must participate in the study, introducing coercion into subject selection. You should not recruit subjects from where you work—especially if you are in a supervisory relationship to them. They may feel that they must participate in your research—which also is coercion.

Think about the goals for your study when choosing your sample participants. If you are recruiting your subjects from a church, then the fact that the subjects are church-members needs to be an important component to your research, because these subjects may not hold views representative of a general population. In fact, this would likely introduce a source of bias into your study and must, at the very least, be addressed in the limitations section of your dissertation. On the other hand, you may not want subjects who are from the general population. If you are interested in doctors, conducting your study in the street will likely not yield you many subjects who are doctors.

Assume that no one will want to participate in your study. In general, people are not anxious to be study subjects. Think about how many times you have deleted a survey request via email from a company, or have avoided the person on the street with the clipboard that you know will ask you to complete a questionnaire. Always assume that no one will be as excited or interested in your study as you are. You really are the only person that has a vested interest in finishing your study. Consider if you can afford to offer incentives for participation, like a small gift card for coffee, etc. Small incentives can do wonders for participation.

When you discuss your subject recruitment you must include all information regarding how you are planning to obtain your subjects. Where are these individuals going to be found? Are they in a school, in the military, working in a particular agency? Will you contact them via flyers, email, or in person? What inclusion and exclusion criteria will you use to decide whether individuals are eligible to participate?

It can be difficult to obtain certain classes of subjects; for example, teachers through school districts, or police officers through police departments. School districts and police departments may be very reluctant to have their people participate. However, it can be much easier to obtain subjects through national or regional associations. Rather than try to obtain your teacher-subjects through the local middle-school, contact your state's teachers' association and find out how you may post a call for subjects in their e-newsletter or on their website.

Subjects and secondary data analysis. If you are utilizing secondary data for your study, you will not need to recruit subjects. This is one of the reasons why using secondary data can be quite a time-saver. What you will need to do in the case of secondary data is to describe how the subjects for the original study were recruited, or—if you are using data that was originally collected for other purposes (for example, patient records created by a hospital system)—then you will need to describe how that data was originally compiled.

Data collection summary for dissertation Chapter 3—research using original data. A key section of the Chapter 3 is the data collection section; in this section, you must describe—in detail—exactly how you plan on collecting your data. This should be detailed in a step-by-step fashion that describes:

- Your research site (where you will be collecting data—not all research has a research site)
- Your subjects, and how you will recruit them
- What your subjects will be going through during the data collection process

Your Research Site. If a research site is being used, you first will need to secure permission from the appropriate individual or office at that site. In some cases, a research site may have their own Institutional Review Board (IRB) to which you will need to submit the appropriate paperwork for approval to conduct your research on their premises. For example, many hospitals and universities have their own IRBs. Don't assume your site will allow you to use it for research, make some calls and see what is involved in getting permission. Do this early in your dissertation work. If you will not be able to use a site, you need to have a contingency plan in place or you may need to shift your focus completely. It is better to find this out early.

Your subjects. You need to first explain who your subjects are and then tell how they will be recruited. We discussed this in depth in the "Who Should Be In The Study?" section.

What your subjects will be going through. You will detail the method that you are employing to collect the data; for example, "Subjects will respond to an online survey of 25 questions. They will be able to complete the survey wherever they choose. Prior to completion, subjects will complete an informed consent form apprising them of their rights. It should take approximately 15 minutes to complete the survey."

Data collection summary for dissertation Chapter 3—employing secondary data. If you are using secondary data, you will need to detail the following:

Explain how the data was originally collected

Explain how you obtained the data from the owner of the data

Explain what portion of the whole original data set is being used

Explain why you chose that portion of the data set

Data analysis. It is beyond the scope of this text to present an exhaustive discussion of data analysis. Once you decide upon the methodology you will use in your study, you must read the literature and educate yourself about the proper data analysis approach. We will provide you with the briefest of overviews so that you can get a feel for what you will be doing during the data analysis stage of your research.

Regardless of which methodology you are employing—quantitative or qualitative—your data must be analyzed in the dissertation, although they are analyzed in very different ways. In your data analysis section of Chapter 3, you will present a step-by-step breakdown outlining how you will analyze your data. This is done for two key reasons: First, it gives you a clear path to follow during your data analysis; and second, it allows other researchers to clearly see what you have done—in case they wish to replicate your study or build a similar study. Remember that your study must fit into the overall context of the academic literature in your field and on your topic.

Quantitative data analysis. In quantitative dissertations, the analysis is all about the statistics you are performing—and there are many different statistics from which to choose.

Descriptive data analysis. Descriptive data analysis in quantitative research usually amounts to the presentation of descriptive statistics, such as the mean and the standard deviation. These will describe to the reader what the data look like and the people who comprise the sample.

Correlational data analysis. Some researchers consider correlation to be descriptive in nature because no manipulation of variables is conducted. In a correlation study, you will be performing either a correlation statistic or some form of a regression analysis that allows you to examine relationships between variables.

Causal-comparative/quasi-experimental data analysis. A t-test, which looks at group differences when there are two groups, is one of the common statistics performed in these types of studies. Other group comparison statistics are also common, like ANOVAs, which allow you to look at group differences when you have more than two groups, ANCOVAs (Analysis of Covariance), and MANOVAs (Multiple Analysis of Variance).

Experimental data analysis. A variety of statistics can be used in experimental data analysis, including an ANOVA (Analysis of variance) and regression. The statistics that are chosen will depend upon whether the data that was collected are nominal, ordinal, interval, or ratio-level data. Students in the social sciences rarely conduct experiments of this nature; this type of study is more commonly employed in the physical sciences.

Qualitative data analysis. Perhaps the most challenging aspect of writing the qualitative dissertation is analyzing the data. The way you conduct your qualitative data analysis will depend upon the qualitative design you have chosen for your study. Phenomenological data is analyzed very differently from Case Study data or Narrative data. It is beyond the scope of this text to present a definitive discussion on how data in each type of qualitative study is analyzed, but a brief overview is presented here.

Case study data analysis. The work of Robert E. Stake can be very helpful for anyone using a case study approach for research. The goal of the case study is—of course—to describe or explain the case that is being studied.

There are two general hallmarks in every case study: the bounded system and triangulation. If you are considering a case study, the object of your research should be some sort of "bounded system"—for example, a work setting or classroom, or a particular event. The boundaries of any case study should be very clear; this lets you know what should be included in your case study and what should be excluded. For example, if you are interested in the topic "perceptions of violence in hospital emergency departments," then you know that your data will focus on emergency departments and not the ICU or the pediatric department; the work environment of the emergency department bounds the study. Multiple types of data are collected in a case study; this is referred to as "triangulation." Through triangulation, a multidimensional picture of what is occurring within the case study is created.

How case study data is analyzed, naturally, depends upon which types of data were collected. If interview data is being used, there are a variety of analytical approaches to choose among. The most common approach is to conduct a thematic analysis, where the interview data is analyzed to see what "themes" are discussed by the subjects. For example, if the research centered around "why people volunteer," themes that might arise upon analysis of the interview data could be "personal gratification," "wanting to give back," and "wanting to feel needed."

Phenomenological data analysis. In a phenomenological study, the researcher is looking for "meaning units" and "themes" to make sense of the experience of the subject. The analysis begins with the researcher "coding" the data, which then allows analyses to follow from that categorization. Amedeo Giorgi is a great source for phenomenological data analysis, as is Clark Moustakas. *Naturalistic Inquiry* by Yvonna Lincoln and Egon Guba is also quite helpful.

Ethnographic data analysis. Much of the analysis in an ethnographic study is organizational—the organization of field notes, interviews, and/or public documents. There really is no single "correct" way to analyze data in an ethnographic study. The researcher may look for patterns within the data; some researchers will create typologies—or categorization. Typologies are common in psychology (for example, personality types). Another technique that can be employed is the creation of a sociogram—a graphic representation of the social links and relationships within the group that is being studied. It can be much easier to present data visually than in writing—especially when the data has very complex relationships contained within it. (See Agar, M. *The professional stranger: an informal introduction to ethnography.*)

Grounded theory data analysis. A variety of methods of data collection can be used in grounded theory—from interviewing to reviewing historical documents. The data analysis will depend upon what types of data are being reviewed. In general, the process of grounded theory flows from identifying codes, to identifying concepts, then to categories, and—finally—creating a theory. The works of Glaser, Strauss and Corbin should be reviewed by anyone considering a grounded theory study.

Narrative data analysis. Because narrative research is all about the story that an individual tells, the analysis of narrative data is concerned with organizing and making sense of that story. Stories may be analyzed structurally or they may be analyzed to get at the meaning that the subject was trying to convey. In some cases, you will perform a content analysis on the data.

Ethical considerations. There are ethical considerations that must be addressed in regard to any research study—even those utilizing secondary data. Ethical considerations can arise from:

- The category of subjects in the study—especially if they are from a vulnerable population (like children or prisoners)
- Who the researcher is in relation to the subjects (for example, if there is a prior relationship between researcher and subject, especially if that relationship is one in which the researcher has a more powerful position than the subject—such as: doctor-patient, therapist-client, employee-supervisor)
- The identity of the researcher—particularly if the researcher has a vested interest in the outcome of the study, or is collecting data from his or her own workplace

In a secondary data study, most ethical concerns arise from the storage and handling of the data, and how the results of the analyses are presented. We will discuss ethical concerns in greater detail in the topic "Preparing for the Institutional Review Board."

Methodology Worksheet

Fill out the worksheet below detailing your methodology.

1. My methodology is _____

2. My design is _____

3. My research questions are

    - _____
    - _____
    - _____
    - _____
    - _____
    - _____

4. My variables for each of my research questions are (list Independent Variables first and Dependent Variables second):

    - _____
    - _____
    - _____
    - _____
    - _____
    - _____

5. These are the main methodological references I will be using to inform my study (note: this is only a starting point, I recommend no fewer than 25 methodological references for any dissertation work):

    - _____
    - _____
    - _____
    - _____

6. I will use the following method(s) to collect data:

    - _____
    - _____
    - _____

7. My subjects will be (be specific!):

    - _____
    - _____
    - _____

8. These are the steps I will take to recruit my subjects:

- _____
- _____
- _____
- _____
- _____

9. These are the steps in my data collection:

- _____
- _____
- _____
- _____
- _____

10. These are the steps in my data analysis:

- _____
- _____
- _____
- _____
- _____

11. These are the ethical considerations related to my study (You will want to return to this after you have read the topic "Preparing for the Institutional Review Board"):

- _____
- _____
- _____
- _____
- _____

Topic: Feasibility Issues

Feasibility must be considered in any dissertation. Feasibility examines how easy, or difficult, it will be to complete a study. Feasibility issues can arise at all junctures of research—from the selection of the topic to data collection—and it is not so much of a matter of whether or not the study is an interesting idea or addresses a gap in the literature, but whether the study can *actually* be carried out in a timely and cost-effective manner. The following are some critical junctures at which issues of feasibility can crop up:

- Study is too broad in scope: would require a multitude of data types to carry out or is really a broad social problem rather than a research problem
- Study will take too long to carry out—for example, a longitudinal study
- Subjects will be difficult to locate or may not readily participate in research
- Subjects are members of a protected and/or vulnerable population
- Topic deals with immoral, illegal, or unusual activities and subjects may be unwilling to discuss them
- The topic of the dissertation is a topic that subjects are unlikely to participate in because of the personal nature of what is being asked (for example, research concerning sexual behavior)
- Research might harm the subjects—either physically or psychologically
- The study is more than minimal risk but does not offer more than minimal benefit, so the IRB is unlikely to approve
- The research questions will be difficult to answer because they are too broad, too vague, or contain ill-defined variables
- The study will require considerable funds to carry out, and the dissertation is unfunded and you do not have the extra cash to put into the study
- Permission from a specific site is required and that site is unlikely to provide permission—for example, schools, police departments, prisons
- Permission will be required from multiple sites

Topic: Secondary Data

Secondary data is data that has previously been collected. There are two types of secondary data: data that has been collected by previous research studies, and data that has been collected for reasons other than research. Secondary data is raw data that has either been collected by another researcher (or team of researchers), or data that was created or assembled in the course of some other activity—for example, information collected by an agency in the course of doing business. We will discuss each of these types separately.

Data Collected Through Previous Research

Data that has been collected in a previous research studies is generally made available to other researchers by federal mandate. This mandate states that if federal funding has been used for a research study, then the data resultant from that study *must* be made reasonably available to other researchers. By requiring this, the federal government assures that it is getting the most "bang for its buck." There are considerable benefits to using this type of secondary data for your dissertation study. First, the government has often invested significant amounts of money—anywhere from tens of thousands to millions of dollars in the original study; most dissertation writers will never have this sort of money to back primary research in their own studies. If the government has already invested the money in the collection of this data, you can take advantage of this and have the resource of all of that money behind your dissertation data as well. Another significant advantage of utilizing secondary data from a large government-funded study is that such studies generally have been designed by not just one Ph.D., but often teams of individuals with Ph.D.s who have years of research experience. Further, in order to obtain government funding, the research proposals had to compete with numerous other studies—and only the best study proposals receive grant funding. If you are able to do so, allow this significant funding put into data collection, and the experience of numerous individuals with terminal degrees, to help you through your dissertation.

Data Collected Without Research

The other type of secondary data is created by agencies or organizations in the normal course of doing business. These data collections can range from the standard psychological battery of tests given to inmates when they enter the correctional system, to the math and reading scores kept by schools. There is plenty of this type of secondary data out there—but a researcher needs to keep in mind that this data was not collected for research purposes and generally does not meet the rigor of data collected for research. You are more likely to run into missing data, lack of standardized definitions for data, and carelessness with this sort of data. Also, because this data is usually owned by the agency that creates it, they may not allow you to use it—or, if they do allow you to use it, but they do not support the findings of your study, they may prevent you from publishing it.

Benefits of Secondary Data

Using secondary data in your dissertation offers significant benefits:
- Saving time, effort, and money;
- Original study was well-designed and well-conducted;
- Many data points collected;
- May contain longitudinal data;

- Provide access to difficult-to-reach populations;
- Alleviate feasibility issues;
- Alleviate ethical issues.

Saving time, effort and money. Collecting *primary* data—regardless of whether you would conduct a quantitative or qualitative study—this takes time, effort and perhaps even money. If you utilize secondary data, you will not need to collect data at all, but you will need to obtain permission to use the secondary data set from its owner. Be sure to determine early on who owns the data set—some data sets are publicly available, some are owned by the institution where the research was conducted, and others are held by government agencies.

Well-designed and well-conducted. If you utilize secondary data that comes from a large government-funded study you also have the benefit of knowing that the research went through a very lengthy and rigorous process of review prior to receiving funding. A single doctoral student did not design it with the help of several dissertation committee members, but a whole team of seasoned researchers designed it, so you know that the original study and data collection were well done.

Many data points collected. The significant funding that large studies receive also allows them to collect a wide variety of data points that would not be possible for a lone researcher to collect. Some studies include data from thousands of participating subjects.

May contain longitudinal data. These studies may have collected data over time and allow you to access longitudinal data that otherwise—during the course of a dissertation—would not be possible or feasible for you to collect.

Provide access to tough to difficult-to-reach populations. These studies can often access populations that would not be accessible to a doctoral student, such as the large epidemiological studies that have been conducted at universities. These studies can look at a variety of diseases or chemical exposures in a large population—which would not be possible for a single, unfunded researcher to do. These large studies may also provide data from vulnerable populations, such as children or prisoners. These studies can also provide data from geographically isolated or remote populations.

Alleviate feasibility issues. If the topic you were considering presented feasibility issues, the use of secondary data can get around these. Many of the benefits previously mentioned addressed feasibility issues—including access to vulnerable populations, access to large amounts of data that will allow you to use more powerful statistics, and access to longitudinal data. Using secondary data will also lessen the time constraints on your research.

Alleviate ethical issues. Because there is no contact with human subjects, secondary data studies have very few ethical concerns—even if the data was collected from a protected population, the ethical issues were vetted prior to the initial data collections.

Drawbacks of Secondary Data

There are a number of drawbacks to the utilization of secondary data that must be noted. There are more concerns—and they are more serious—for secondary data that was not originally generated for research purposes; these include:

- No control over data collection; no control over the population;
- No control over the variables in the study or how they were measured;
- Limitations in the design and statistics.

No control over data collection. The heading kind of says it all: you have had no control over *how* the data was collected, and must rely on the intentions of the original data collectors. If your secondary data is coming from a large government-funded study, you have fewer concerns in this area. However, if your secondary data was created in another way (by an agency or organization in the course of doing business) then you may have some serious concerns to address in this area; it is not uncommon to find missing, confusing, or even contradictory data in secondary data that has been drawn from an agency. Employees who input information for their jobs—not for research—are not thinking of "completeness of the data," or "operational definitions of the data," they are merely *doing their jobs* and aren't likely to be as concerned about incomplete or cohesiveness of data. We have seen more than one dissertation hit a snag because agency data—while useful for that agency—was not very useful or complete enough for the sake of research. While these students did finish their dissertations, the product that they produced was not very useful in the field—except, that is, to caution others about the use of agency-created data.

No control over the population. In any secondary data study, you have no control over the study population. For example, if you are interested in how older individuals respond to evacuation orders during a hurricane, and the large dataset only has 20 people over the age of 60 included in it, then you clearly cannot use it for your study, as 20 individuals cannot be deemed a representative population.

No control over variables or how they were measured. You have no control over the variables that are included in the original study or how those variables were defined and measured. You can only ask questions of the data that were originally asked. For example, if there is no measure of depression in the original study, you cannot use depression as a variable in your study. Not only are limited in your choice of variables by those that were included in the original study, but you are also limited by *how* the variables were measured. If depression was included as a variable in the original study but the only way it was measured was by the inclusion of one question: "Are you depressed?" then you need to use this very unreliable and "unclinical" measure of depression. You do not have the option of using a normed, validated instrument (like the "Beck Depression Inventory") to measure depression because the original data collection did not include a normed, validated instrument.

You can only take information out of the data that *is in* the data. If a variable that you require was not included in the study, then the data is useless to you—unless you restructure your study. Because of how much time you will save using reliable secondary data, this is something that you should consider. You are limited in your choice of variables by those that were included in the original study, so use variables that are in the secondary data set. In the long run, it is much easier than collecting your own data.

Limitations in design and use of statistics. You generally cannot use an experimental approach when you utilize secondary data. If you were interested in analyzing data across time (longitudinally) and that was not done in the original study, then you simply cannot use the data in that manner. You also generally cannot combine two or more datasets to find the variables that you want because in the majority of cases, data from different individuals is included in those datasets and cannot be cross-compared.

Why You May Have Never Thought of Secondary Data Before

Many dissertation writers never even consider the possibility of utilizing secondary data for their dissertation research. It is not even discussed in some doctoral programs. Some professors may object to secondary data on philosophical grounds, feeling that if the doctoral student is truly being trained to be a researcher, that the student should engage in all parts of the research process, including data collection.

Steps in Doing a Secondary Data Analysis Study

The process of completing a dissertation utilizing secondary data is not significantly different from the dissertation process that we have already discussed. Most of the early steps, such as topic selection and writing the literature review do not change at all. However, there are some special considerations for your methodology: A number of the steps are shortened or eliminated completely, and little is added to the process when secondary data is utilized.

Topic selection. Secondary data can help you choose the topic for your dissertation. You may be working with a faculty member on his or her research or even on a large research study helping to collect data. This would be an excellent place to find your topic, since you likely are already familiar with the data.

The literature review. There are no significant changes to the literature review portion of your study. Regardless of whether you are collecting primary data or utilizing secondary data, you will do the same work.

Select a dataset. This is one of the steps that utilizing secondary data will add to your dissertation process. Once you have determined the general topic area in which you are interested, you need to look at potential data sets. Keep in mind that while many data sets are free, that others are not. Be sure to inquire. But don't let cost deter you. A good data set that you spend a hundred dollars for can save you weeks or months of work.

You will need to spend considerable time studying the codebook for the dataset in which you are interested. The codebook will detail how the data was collected, what variables were included, how they were measured and how each was coded.

You will also need to determine who owns the data set and how you obtain permission to utilize the data set. Some data sets are publicly owned—utilizing one of these will not present a problem. So that you do not run into stumbling blocks with access when you go through IRB, you should find the answers to these questions early on in the process.

The methodology. In most instances, a secondary data analysis study will be a quantitative study. Generally, the spirit of qualitative studies precludes a secondary data approach—you may use historical data (newspapers, diaries, letters) for a qualitative study, but you generally would not utilize someone else's interview data—as that pretty much goes against the whole philosophy behind qualitative research.

The design. When you utilize a secondary data set, the types of data that were collected in that data set limit your design. In general, experimental designs will not be available to you, but quasi-experimental designs are possible as is a correlational design.

The variables or concepts in secondary data. You will be limited in your choice of variables to those that were collected in the original study. Of course, if a particular variable was not collected in the original study, you cannot use that variable. Or if a variable was collected in one particular way, there is nothing you can do to change that. For example, if you would like age to be a whole number, but the data set collected age as a range, then you are stuck with age as a range—and it may be difficult to run certain statistics, meaningful to your study, using that variable.

The research questions. The research questions that you write must include variables that were actually collected in the study. If you had other research questions in mind, you must set them aside and create research questions that utilize the variables in the data set. It is easier generally to rewrite research questions than it is to collect your own data.

The methods. When using secondary data, study the methods that were utilized to collect the data—the methods that were chosen by the original data collectors. Of course, you have no control over them, but you still must describe the methods that were originally used to collect the data in the methodology section of your dissertation. You also must describe how you chose the portion of the original data set for your own study.

Subjects. Because the data has already been collected, you, of course, do not need to recruit subjects: you need only discuss how the subjects were originally recruited. This is quite a benefit if you are interested in a vulnerable population, which can be very difficult to access for novice researchers. Not having to recruit subjects will also save time and effort. In the same manner as the methods employed for data collection, in a secondary data study you have no control over the subjects that were chosen for the original study. If the population you want to look at was not included, then there is nothing you can do about it.

Data collection. This step in the process changes from a primary-data-collection dissertation. In your data collection section, you will explain:

- How the data was originally collected
- How you obtained the data from the owner of the data
- What portion of the whole original data set is being used
- Why you chose that portion of the data set

Data analysis. Someone collected secondary data other than you, and that person (or committee) made choices about how the data was collected and how the variables were defined, and this will limit the types of analyses that you can perform on the data. You will be able to present descriptive statistics on the data. In general, causal relationships cannot be examined using secondary data. If data was collected as categorical data rather than non-categorical data, you will not be able to perform higher-level statistics. On the plus side, however, there are often more subjects in a secondary data set, so this will allow you to perform your quantitative statistics (when otherwise you might be very limited in what analyses you could perform) across a broader group of representative subjects than you would have been able to collect on your own.

Ethical considerations. There are far fewer ethical concerns in a study that utilizes de-identified (meaning all identifiers have already been removed from the data) secondary data. If you are using a de-identified secondary data set you will qualify for an exempt IRB review. This is the briefest of IRB reviews and does not require the full IRB committee to review the proposal. Research falling under this type of review is of minimal risk to subjects. The only ethical concerns that arise in a secondary data study revolve around the storage, handling, and write-up of the data. Data must be protected at all times, and should not be given to unauthorized persons. The write up of the data should not be done it a way that will harm the original subjects.

The Remainder of the Dissertation Process

There will be very few other changes to the dissertation process. In your results chapter, you need to reiterate much of your methods discussion from the methodology chapter. The owners of the data set may also require that you let them know when your dissertation is published so that they can provide access to it on their website, this is commonly done—as you will notice when searching for a data set, they often list all studies published from the data set.

Topic: Writing Chapter 1

It may seem counter-intuitive to discuss writing Chapter 1 so far into this text—it may seem as though it should be written much earlier. This was done intentionally, however as Chapter 1—the introduction to the dissertation (or the proposal, if you are in the proposal-writing stage)—really should be written *last*. It is easiest if it is written last.

Chapter 1 will lead your reader through the entirety of your proposal or dissertation. You are telling them, in brief, what you will tell them, at length, in the remainder of the dissertation. Keep in mind that Chapter 1 should be perfectly aligned with all of the other chapters in the dissertation—in other words, it should present no surprises. The literature that you mention briefly here is the literature that you explore in great detail in Chapter 2; the variables that you mention here are the same variables that you discuss in Chapter 3.

Writing Chapter 1 for the Proposal

Chapter 1 will begin by presenting the purpose of your dissertation—the research problem that you will be investigating. It will provide a brief synopsis of the literature review; it will provide an overview of your methodology.

Writing Chapter 1 for the Dissertation

Chapter 1 in the dissertation presents all of the same information that chapter 1 for the proposal does, except the writing changes to past tense—because the study has been conducted—and you will also present an overview of the results (chapter 4) and the discussion (chapter 5). Because of its nature in informing the reader of what is being presented in all the future chapters, it is logical that this summation can be most easily assembled after those other parts have been written.

Topic: Preparing for the Institutional Review Board

Institutional Review Boards (IRBs) are federally mandated to oversee research and protect human subjects. IRBs are in place at Universities and other organizations such as hospitals. There are also privately run IRBs. Your university's IRB will look at your research proposal to ensure that it will not cause harm to your subjects, in particular, or to any class of individuals, in general. The IRB also serves to protect you, as the researcher, both legally and physically, and also to protect the university, legally.

The IRB is made up of a committee of individuals. Many of the individuals will have a background in science, however, all IRBs must also have at least one person who is a non-scientist community representative. If an IRB will review research dealing with vulnerable populations there must be an individual who can serve as a representative for those individuals who is a part of that IRB. For example, if your research deals with children, one of the people who review your research proposal will have specialized experience working with children.

The best way to get through the IRB is to give serious consideration to the possible ethical issues that might be contained within your research. In particular, you need to consider ethical issues from a research standpoint. For example, individuals who work with prisoners on a daily basis often do not consider them to be "vulnerable," but as far as research is concerned, they are.

Consider the following questions:
- Is there benefit in your research?
    o All IRBs will look at a potential study to make sure that there is scientific merit to the study: that it—at least in some small way—advances the discipline, and that it is a well-crafted study.
    o If you study is low-risk there does not need to be a significant benefit; however, if you have a higher level of risk in your study, then there correspondingly must also be greater benefit. Generally speaking, social science dissertations must be low-risk because they are low-benefit.
- Is there the potential for harm in your research?
    o The IRB will look for the potential of physical harm to you or to your subjects. For example, if you wanted to go to offenders' homes to collect data, the IRB would very likely consider that to be too much of a risk to your safety to approve.
    o The IRB will also look for the potential of psychological or emotional harm to potential research subjects—which is the most common factor for concern in studies. It is unlikely that an IRB will allow a dissertation-level researcher to work with subjects who are more likely to be harmed unless you have special training or experience, and that you put into place special precautions to guard against harm (for example, individuals who have been victims of violent crimes, individuals with post traumatic stress disorder, individuals who have attempted suicide),
- Does your research deal with subjects who are vulnerable?
    o Ethical concerns in research studies can revolve around the subjects if the subjects are from a vulnerable population (for example, children, prisoners, cognitively impaired individuals). It can be difficult to collect

primary data from vulnerable populations; in such cases, searching for a secondary data source may be the only viable alternative.

- Is it obvious that certain individuals or sites are being used in your research?
  - It is important that the identities of your research subjects and research sites remain anonymous and that they cannot be associated with particular statistics/statements/opinions in you published dissertation. Make sure no one and no site can be identified or gleaned from what you have written.
- Are you somehow involved in a dual relationship with your subjects?
  - Dual relationships are not allowed between researcher and subject primarily because of the potential for coercion and bias. Dual relationships may arise between teacher-student, therapist-client, doctor-patient and so forth. If the researcher is in the dominant position over the potential subject, then coercion may be present. If the researcher is using his or her own clients for research, the researcher has a vested interest in the outcome of the study. IRBs also are reluctant to allow researchers to collect data where they work.
- Does the possibility for coercion exist in your study?
  - The IRB will look for the possibility of coercion in your study. The IRB will also look at whether or not the remuneration offered in the study could be coercive. For a poor or homeless individual, ten dollars might be considered coercive, whereas for a mid-level executive, $100 would not be considered coercive.
- Are you utilizing secondary data for your study?
  - The utilization of secondary data will circumvent many IRB issues. These studies generally qualify for an exempt review. Since you will not be interacting with subjects, the study is deemed to be low-risk. You are also able to utilize secondary data from vulnerable populations—which may be the only way for you to conduct research with these populations. No consent materials will be required. The IRB will be interested in whether or not you can obtain access to the data, and it will still look at the scientific merit of the study.

Topic: The Proposal and Proposal Defense

In most schools, the dissertation proposal consists of the first three chapters of the dissertation: the introduction, the literature review and the methodology. Your committee will read and provide comments on your proposal; when they are satisfied with what you have written, you may be expected to formally defend your proposal. Proposal defenses are handled in different ways—for some departments and chairs, the defense is a rubber stamp, whereas for others it is a very rigorous process; other departments do not conduct proposal defenses at all. If your school does conduct proposal defenses, you should do some of your own investigative work to see how they are generally handled. You may even be able to attend a proposal defense if one is being held prior to you reaching that stage of your doctoral work. Once you have a dissertation chair, you should ask what to expect, how he or she normally handles the defense.

The proposal defense will generally take place after you have received IRB approval and immediately prior to authorization to begin data collection. You should be prepared to present your proposed research, in brief during your defense. You may need to prepare handouts, a PowerPoint presentation, and/or a lecture. You will also likely have to respond to questions about your proposed research; these questions will revolve around theory, design, the literature review, and feasibility issues. In many departments, the proposal defense is also an opportunity for you to ask any questions that you have—remember that everyone on your committee has conducted research and it is part of their job as committee members to guide you through yours.

Preparing for the Proposal Defense

The questions below are designed to help prepare you for your defense. If you have used this text to guide you through the dissertation process, you should have no problem answering them.

Theory. You should be prepared to respond to questions like the following during your defense:

1. Why did you choose the theory in your proposal?

    _____

    _____

    _____

2. What other theories have been considered?

    _____

    _____

    _____

3. Why were those theories not chosen?

    _____

    _____

    _____

4. How does your theory inform your choice of variables?

    _____

    _____

    _____

5. How will your theory inform your data analysis?

    _____

    _____

    _____

6. How does your research contribute to the theory literature?

    _____

    _____

    _____

Design. You should be prepared to answer the following questions about your design:

1. Why did you choose to conduct a quantitative/qualitative study?

    _____

    _____

    _____

2. Why are the variables in your study important?

    _____

    _____

    _____

3. Why did you choose this statistic or qualitative design?

    _____

    _____

    _____

4. What other design options have you considered for this study?

    _____

    _____

    _____

5. Why were those options not pursued?

    _____

    _____

    _____

6. How is your design better than other possible options?

    _____

    _____

    _____

Literature review. It can be difficult to predict what sort of questions you will be asked about your literature review. This is generally a very individualized part of the dissertation and questions often will revolve around what you should or should not include in this portion of your dissertation. Make sure that you have done a very thorough literature review. This will also need to be updated once you complete the final dissertation to account for any studies that have been published in the interim.

Feasibility. You should be prepared to answer the following questions:

1. If you cannot reach your desired number of participants using your proposed plan for recruitment, what is your backup plan?

    _____

    _____

2. If this a vulnerable population or the study is more than minimal risk, what precautions have you put into place to protect your subjects?

_____

_____

_____

3. How long do you anticipate it will take you to collect your data?

_____

_____

_____

Topic Cluster: Monitoring

Monitoring consists of watching for potential pitfalls and keeping track of the how the dissertation is progressing. During the monitoring stage, you will also identify possible corrective actions that need to be taken to get you back on track. Unfortunately, most dissertation students—even those that are academically well-prepared for the dissertation—do not adequately monitor their dissertation process; nor are they aware of what could potentially go wrong. This may be because the whole process is so overwhelming and you easily become swamped, or it may be because you are so busy focusing on the small details of the dissertation that you lose track of the big picture. Serious delays may happen when "unexpected events" occur, or when even very little things go wrong. The majority of the battle against such delays lies simply in understanding what could go wrong, and in being prepared to take corrective action.

Topic: Taking Feedback Without Taking it Personally

Of all of the academic work that you have done, the dissertation will pose the greatest challenge. You will be required to write and rewrite portions of your dissertation. We have known students who have had to rewrite the dissertation from beginning to end. Repeated rewrites of chapters four and five are very common. The one shared personality trait that all successful dissertation students—with "successful" meaning that they have finished—is that they were able to take the feedback given to them and use it to create a better dissertation. They did not see feedback as a negative, but rather as a gift—something positive designed to make them grow and make their dissertation a better product.

Unfortunately, having gotten all "A's" in your coursework at the doctoral level will neither prepare you for a dissertation, nor will it guarantee your success. Most faculty who teach doctoral level classes do not fail students, in fact, many of them do not even give Cs. Do not take your GPA as an indication of how prepared you are for completing a dissertation—it is not a reliable indicator of whether or not you will complete the dissertation, or how smooth the journey may be.

Only about half of all students who enter doctoral studies actually complete their dissertation; while some will drop out during coursework, the majority are lost during the dissertation process. This stems from two challenges: first, a lack of preparation for the dissertation; and second, a lack of knowledge about the dissertation process. The goal of this text is to address both of these challenges.

It is important during the dissertation process to be able to handle criticism and setbacks—even failure. Most people learn more from failure than they do from success. The dissertation pathway is often littered with small failures and setbacks, coupled—by its nature—with lots of feedback. When feedback or criticism is provided, we have seen many students get caught up in defending their work, rather than make the necessary changes. This is not a time to dig your heels in and resist. It is important to use each criticism and setback as an opportunity for growth, and an opportunity to learn more.

It is also vital to separate your work, your writing, and your research from yourself. Feedback on your work, writing or research is *not* a criticism of *you as a person*. Do not identify too closely with what you have produced, or you will find it a greater challenge to grow from the feedback that you are given, and it will be more difficult to use it as a tool for improvement. In other words, don't ever take it personally.

Topic: Stumbling Blocks

We all encounter stumbling blocks during our lives and because of the nature of the dissertation and the rigor that is required, you are all the more likely to encounter stumbling blocks during this period. The most important point to keep in is to not let stumbling blocks prevent you from finishing. Your dissertation should contain stumbling blocks only—not roadblocks. As soon as you come across a stumbling block, you must devise a plan of attack, and overcome it. If something sets you back a week or a month, accept that and move forward—so that the month doesn't turn into a year, and the stumbling block doesn't become a stopping point. Don't worry about the time that you have already lost—just prevent yourself from losing any more time.

There are two types of stumbling blocks in the dissertation process: those that are external to the dissertation process and others that are internal to the dissertation process. External stumbling blocks come from outside the dissertation process—such as issues related to family or work. Internal stumbling blocks arise from the dissertation and the dissertation process itself.

External Stumbling Blocks

We have already discussed many potential external stumbling blocks. Refer back to "Distractions and Setting Priorities" in the Planning Cluster. These stumbling blocks can range from the mundane—like spending too much time watching TV or playing video games instead of working—to the very serious, such as divorce, job loss, or the death of someone close to you. Any distraction can easily become a stumbling block. Luckily, you have already created a way to deal with those stumbling blocks. Refer back to these plans of action any time you need them. If you should come upon a stumbling block that you did not consider previously, repeat the same process that you went through for your other stumbling blocks—it works every time. And if you should encounter a stumbling block that you cannot devise a plan of action for, seek assistance. You can talk to a professional counselor or therapist for personal issues; if it is an issue related to school, you could talk to your advisor. If you don't find the first person knowledgeable about your particular stumbling block, seek out another person until you find someone who can assist you.

When the stumbling block is very serious, you may need to take a step back from the dissertation to deal with what has happened. Allow yourself time to do so—but be sure to set an expectation for when you will return to the dissertation; for example, give yourself a month off—but no more. Make sure that you take enough time to deal with your stumbling block or it may continue to be a problem and you may not be able to regain your concentration on the dissertation. On the other hand, there is the danger that if you allow too much time to pass that you will not be able to return to the dissertation because you have lost all of your momentum and motivation.

Internal Stumbling Blocks

Internal stumbling blocks arise out of the dissertation itself and the dissertation process.

Process in general. Perhaps the most commonly encountered stumbling block encountered during the dissertation is the mystique that surrounds this major piece of research. Hopefully this text will have helped you take care of that stumbling block. After you have read this text, the mystery surrounding the general process of the dissertation should be clearer. We know that many people never finish the dissertation requirement of their doctoral studies, so it is much feared—and fear alone can become a stumbling block. We have seen many dissertation students succumb to the fear of the dissertation and quit. More than anything else, you need to believe in yourself that you can finish—even when it seems impossible.

Subject recruitment. Another stumbling block may be "I cannot recruit enough subjects." But if you refer back to our discussions about subjects and subject recruitment under "The Design" section in the Execution Cluster, you will see that you have already created a back-up plan for obtaining more subjects if your first recruitment attempt is unsuccessful. Also, re-read what you wrote in the "Proposal and Proposal Defense" section.

Site permission. One common stumbling block that students encounter is that they cannot gain access to the research site from which they want to recruit subjects—such as an agency or school; permission is not granted. If your dissertation centers on a particular site, then having that site not allow you to recruit can be devastating. This is one reason why we caution against recruiting subjects through agencies, but rather to recruit them as individuals. If your potential subjects are middle school teachers, rather than try to access them through a particular school district, access them through a professional organization for teachers. In this way, the agency no longer acts as a gatekeeper—but you are still able to access individuals for your research.

Institutional Review Board. While many students see the IRB as a potential stumbling block, in reality, it can be a considerable help to any researcher. Visit your school's IRB webpage early in your research process; you are likely to find useful forms, submission dates, and information here. You can contact your institution's IRB early in the process via email or phone to ask specific questions pertaining to your research.

Quantitative secondary data set problems. Problems can arise in quantitative with secondary data sets. Until we actually obtain the data set, we may not know how many subjects it contains for a particular variable. This will pose a problem for statistical analysis—depending upon the analysis you may need 100 or more data points. In some instances, you must search for a different data set; in others, you might be able to change your inclusion criteria to include more subjects from the total database. If the total database was already small you may need to find another database.

You may also not be able to find the variables that you want to measure in your dataset, or they may not have been measured the way you anticipated. In this case, you can either choose different variables or locate a different data set.

Quantitative statistics issues. Problems can arise in performing the statistics for a quantitative dissertation. If you find that you are having difficulties completing the statistics or using a statistical package, you may want to consider taking a statistics class at your local community college or at your own university. MOOCs (Massive Open Online Courses) also offer a free alternative solution to paying to take a class. And you can always hire a statistics tutor to help—if your university allows that.

Qualitative interview problems. Qualitative interviewing is a skill—and it can prove a difficult skill to acquire during the dissertation process. In most qualitative research, everything centers upon the interview process and the rich verbal data that you get from the interviews. If you are not getting rich data during your interviews, then your analysis may become seriously compromised because there will literally be very little to analyze. A beneficial way to make sure that you are obtaining rich interview data is to have your dissertation chair listen to your interview tapes or read your transcripts. If your chair checks your interviews early on—for example, after the first two or three interviews—interview problems can be caught early and corrected. Your chair can make specific recommendations to obtain more robust interviews—some of which may include reworking your questions, or practicing more listening in your interviews.

Qualitative saturation problems. Qualitative interviews are generally conducted until saturation is reached—which means that new subjects are repeating what previous subjects have already told us. Problems can occur when saturation is reached too early in the interview process, which may also leave us with too little data to analyze. (This can indicate that our topic of choice perhaps should have been explored quantitatively rather than qualitatively.) On the other hand, we may fail to reach saturation—and not know if we have thoroughly explored our topic; in this case, we may want to continue interviewing. This can also mean that our chosen topic is too broad and we may need to narrow our focus.

Qualitative data not rich enough. In qualitative research, stumbling blocks commonly arise when the data is not rich enough for analysis. If your interviews are not yielding rich data, then you may need to revisit your interview questions and edit them so that they elicit fuller responses from the subjects. In some cases—in qualitative—when you were going to review existing documents, those documents may not be as fruitful as you originally thought. In that case, you need to present what you can from that data and hopefully there are enough other data points in your study to make up for lack in one type of data. This can be particularly tricky, and is one of the key reasons why we spend so much time preparing the design phase of a qualitative study.

Writing. Writing often poses a stumbling block for students in dissertation. Even for a solid writer—who has written or even published academic papers—writing a full book (which is what the dissertation is) can be very challenging. After reading this text, you should be able to break your writing down into smaller pieces, which will make the task more manageable. For students who are poor writers or who lack the foundation of good grammar, usage, and mechanics, the writing of the dissertation poses a much greater problem. It is very important that you use whatever tools your university has provided to obtain an honest and critical assessment of your writing (remember what we said earlier about accepting feedback and criticism), and then to use that assessment to improve your writing. It can be very beneficial to take a technical writing class. There really is no other way to improve your writing than to write.

Topic Cluster: Closing

Closing, of course, is the ending of the project—at this point, the end of the dissertation is now in sight. It will involve writing the results chapter, writing the discussion chapter, the final editing of the dissertation, defending the dissertation, and preparing for the last administrative steps involved in graduation. During closing, you will also begin to consider what you will do with the dissertation after graduation, and what you will be doing with yourself after you graduate..

Topic: Writing the Results Chapter—Chapter 4

Timeline Reminder

The timeline presented earlier in this text suggests two weeks for quantitative data collection and 3–6 months for qualitative data collection. These timeframes are rough estimates. Since secondary data eliminates this step, the time will be lessened to almost zero for secondary data studies and will only take as long as it does to secure the dataset. For some qualitative studies—such as ethnographies—it can take years to collect the data. The estimation of the time to collect data can also be lengthened if it proves difficult to obtain subjects for either a qualitative or quantitative dissertation.

The writing of Chapter 4 should take between one and two months, with the possibility of the qualitative write-up taking considerably longer. Results chapters for quantitative dissertations are generally much easier to write because they will all follow a similar format depending upon the type of analyses that were performed; it is a good idea to find some examples from your department of results chapters that were written for the analyses (for example, Regression or MANOVA) you have chosen and use these as templates for your own results chapter. Results chapters for qualitative dissertations are much more challenging to write; again, it's a good idea to look at a variety of dissertations that utilized the qualitative approach you have chosen (phenomenology or case study, for example) and to use their subheadings as guidance for your own. Your timeline devoted to writing may be shortened if you are a very strong writer and might need to be lengthened if your writing is not strong.

Tools Reminder

Perhaps the most useful tool for writing Chapter 4 is the outline. As we have mentioned, you can construct potential outlines from the subheadings you find in other dissertations—this can be done for both quantitative and qualitative dissertations, although the qualitative dissertation will be much more individualized depending upon your design and the topic of your dissertation.

What Is the Results Chapter?

Whether you have conducted a quantitative or qualitative study, your results chapter will present the results of your analyses. There is no one correct way to construct the results section, and if you look at a selection of dissertations from your department, you will the results chapter constructed in different ways. As long as it lets the reader know what the results were, it is generally acceptable.

Quantitative Results Chapter

The quantitative results chapter will present appropriate descriptive and inferential statistics—this may include tables, charts and graphs depending upon the data. The main point is to walk the reader through the results of your analyses. Like all chapters, you will begin with an introduction and end with a conclusion. It may be beneficial to create subheadings for each research question, its corresponding hypothesis, null hypothesis, the statistics that were performed, and a discussion of whether or not you were able to reject the null hypothesis. Your subheadings would be as follows:

Example 1 of subheadings for a quantitative chapter 4.

Introduction. This will provide the reader with an introduction to the material that will be presented in this Chapter. For a dissertation, it's a good idea to include an introduction at the beginning of every chapter.

Research question 1. You will present your first research question. You will also present the corresponding hypothesis and null hypothesis. Then you will present the descriptive and other statistics that you used to conduct the analysis for this research question. Finally, discuss whether the statistics support rejection of the null hypothesis or not.

Research question 2. Now you do the same thing for your second research question as you did for your first.

Research question 3. Again, same as your first research question.

Research question 4. Although we have only listed four research questions, this does not imply that you should have only four. You may have fewer—or more. But continue in the same general format until you have presented all of your research questions, their hypotheses, null hypotheses and all of the analyses that were conducted for each.

Conclusion. Close chapter by summarizing what was presented in the chapter. This is a good place to reiterate which null hypotheses you were able to reject and which ones you were not able to reject.

Example 2 of subheadings for a quantitative chapter 4.

You can also choose to utilize subheadings that present first your descriptive statistics and then higher-level statistics. In this case, your subheadings might be:

Introduction. Again, present an introduction to orient the reader to the text that follows.

Descriptive statistics. Descriptive statistics include measures of central tendency, measures of dispersion, and so forth. These are very low-level statistics. Quantitative dissertations should present more than just descriptive statistics.

Inferential statistics. These are higher-level statistics. As the name suggests, it is possible to draw inferences from these statistics. These include regression, ANOVA, correlation, and structural equation modeling.

Conclusion. Remind the reader of what you have just presented. You can also include a segue into the next chapter.

We have also seen results chapters that have no subheadings at all—although we would not recommend this because it can be difficult to write without the guidance and organization that subheadings provide. Generally, as you review other dissertations, you will notice that the subheadings used in the results chapter in quantitative dissertations are fairly straightforward. There is no need for you to do anything different—don't reinvent the wheel. Again, the important thing to remember is that you must present your results clearly, so that the average dissertation reader understands your study.

Qualitative Results Chapter

The qualitative results chapter, like the quantitative results chapter, will discuss how the data was collected and the steps that comprised the data analyses, but there is a much greater variation to the results chapters of qualitative studies. There are many more choices to be made in the organization of a qualitative results chapter. We always recommend beginning with an "Introduction" and ending with a "Conclusion." You may also want to include a section entitled "Credibility," as this is often key in a qualitative dissertation. Including "Description of Sample," is also a good subheading. In some qualitative dissertations, the writer will include a section entitled "Data Analysis Process;" in others, the writer will create subheadings for each step in the data analysis that was laid out in the methodology chapter. This also has the benefit of creating a nice parallel between chapters three and four.

Example 1 of subheadings for a qualitative chapter 4.
- "Textural descriptions"
- "Structural descriptions"
- "Themes"

Example 2 of subheadings for a qualitative chapter 4.
- "Individual textural descriptions"
- "Composite textual description"
- "Composite structural description"
- "Composite textual-structural description"

In a case study, you could choose to create a subheading for each type of data that was collected (remember, there are generally three different types of data collected in a case study)—for example:

Example 3 of subheadings for a qualitative chapter 4.
- "Interview data"
- "Observational data"
- "Data from a structured measure"

Example 1 of subheadings for a qualitative chapter 4.
- "Focus group interview data"
- "Individual interview data"
- "Survey data"

Topic: Writing the Discussion Chapter—Chapter 5

Timeline Reminder

The timeline estimated that it would take approximately one month to write a draft of your final chapter. A word of caution: if you have not been rewriting and editing during the entire dissertation process, it could take considerably longer to write the final chapter.

Tools Reminder

This final chapter is all about good writing and organization. You need to provide a discussion that ties all of the pieces of your dissertation together and builds a bridge to future research.

What is the Discussion Chapter?

The final chapter of the dissertation, the Discussion Chapter, is usually the most enjoyable chapter to write because it focuses on your own research (rather that the academic literature) and directions for the future (rather than what has transpired in the past). It summarizes everything from the previous chapters of the dissertation. The dissertation follows the format, "tell them what you are going to tell them, then tell them the facts, and finally tell them what you told them." You are not just reiterating what you stated in chapter 4, but rather you are presenting broad conclusions from the entire dissertation. While there is considerable variation to the subsections of chapter 5, you may want to address the following in your chapter 5:

- Introduction
- Review of the Results
- Results in Context of the Literature
- Suggestions for Future Research
- Limitations of the Study
- Theoretical Implications
- Policy Implications
- Practical Applications
- Conclusion

Introduction. It should go without stating that you begin each chapter with an introduction to the material presented in that chapter. It may seem highly redundant as you are writing it, but it does help to orient your reader to what will follow.

Review of the results. Even though the Results Chapter is usually the chapter the directly preceding the Discussion Chapter, most dissertations will present a brief overview of the Results Chapter here. Even though it may seem redundant, this is the format that most dissertations follow.

Results in context of the literature. Some dissertations will next discuss the results of the current study into the context of the literature on the topic. This allows you—again—to create that link to previous studies by showing how your study agrees or disagrees with the research that others have conducted.

Suggestions for future research. You must also include "suggestions for future research" in the discussion chapter. Here you will build a bridge to future research on the same topic. If you were full of ideas for studies and very broad topics at the outset of your dissertation journey, you should include some of them here. Include a discussion that centers around how you might redesign your study—or what variables you might include—if you had to do it all over again. You can also talk about what you might have missed in the design process, or interesting things that you discovered during data collection. It is perfectly legitimate to include a discussion of things that you would have liked to have addressed in your study—but didn't. Talk about what the next logical steps are for the progression of the topic's research. If you conducted a qualitative study, do not hesitate to include ideas for potential quantitative studies (and vice versa for quantitative studies)—remember that the research in any discipline is a mixture of quantitative and qualitative and the two approaches complement each other.

Limitations of the study. You may include a subheading "Limitations of the Study"—especially if you have had considerable difficulty at some point during the study: if it was difficult to recruit subjects, if the methodology presented problems, or if you became aware of confounding variables during the study that cast doubt on the conclusions that could be drawn from your research. It is not a sign of weakness or failure to include this information—rather it is a sign of maturity and honest appraisal of the research. This can be especially important to future researchers who may desire to build off of your study as it presents them with concrete ideas of how to redesign your study to make it better.

Theoretical implications. If your dissertation was conducted to test theory—or if the goal of your dissertation was the creation of theory—then you should discuss the theoretical implications of your study. It is not common for students to address theoretical implications, but in some cases it is appropriate.

Policy implications. You may also discuss the policy implications of your research, but be certain you have the necessary background in policy to make appropriate statements—as not all doctoral programs will cover policy in their coursework. If you are going to include a subheading concerning policy, you will want to discuss how your research could inform policy changes at appropriate governmental levels. A healthcare dissertation might have policy implications at the state or federal level, or it might inform the policies of individual hospitals.

Practical applications. You can also discuss the practical, "field-applications" of your study. Take what you have learned from your research and translate it into knowledge that the practitioner could use in the day-to-day performance of his or her job. This is an area that is frequently left out of dissertations, but should be given serious consideration as it helps to bridge the gap between research and practice in a field.

Conclusion. Each chapter will close with a conclusion that succinctly sums up the material that has been presented in the chapter. Again, while this seems redundant, this is the format that dissertation writing follows.

Topic: Final Editing

Your chair and your committee will provide final comments on the entirety of your dissertation and you will do some rewriting. Additionally, all universities have a process in place where your dissertation will be reviewed for general writing issues and also for appropriate formatting—which will vary depending upon the style manual you are using (APA, MLA, Chicago, and so forth). This step is not intended to copy-edit your dissertation, but rather to make sure that it looks appropriate for publication. There is nothing more embarrassing or unprofessional than a dissertation with typos, incorrect grammar and poor formatting. Imagine what that says about you—and your University—to the research world!

If your chair or committee members have made stylistic comments along the way, you should have incorporated the appropriate corrections—this can save you time as you go into the final university process of editing. It is also a good idea to write all of your doctoral level papers in the style appropriate for your discipline. Don't be content to let formatting be an afterthought. If you spend your entire doctoral career formatting your papers correctly, it will not be such a burden to do so when you are writing the dissertation.

Timeline Reminder

The timeline estimated that it would take approximately 1-2 months to redraft the entire dissertation. Because final editing and format-checking is a university-based process, it is difficult to estimate how long that will take, but you can shorten this process by providing them with a very clean copy of your dissertation so that their edits are light. You should also find out well in advance if format-checking can only occur during certain times of the year— for example, only when the semester is in session. This edit will have nothing to do with content, but will be all about format.

Topic: Dissertation Defense

Your committee will read and provide comments on your full dissertation. When they are satisfied with what you have written, you will formally defend your dissertation. The dissertation defense is very much like the proposal defense, except that all departments have some form of a final dissertation defense. Just like the proposal, the final defense can be either a rubber stamp or a real "trial-by-fire." As you did with the proposal defense, you should do some of your own investigative work to see how the final dissertation defense is generally handled in your school. Try to attend someone else's dissertation defense so that you can understand the process going in. (There were a number of other doctoral students in attendance at my own defense, each of whom were within months of finishing up.) Ask your dissertation chair how he or she normally handles the final defense.

In a similar manner to the proposal defense, you should be prepared to answer questions—although the focus now will be on what happened during the research, the challenges you might have faced during the research, and what you might do with the research moving forward.

Preparing for the Final Dissertation Defense

The questions below are designed to help prepare you for your final dissertation defense. If you have used this text to guide you through the dissertation process, you should have no problems answering them.

Theory. You should be prepared to respond to questions like the following during your defense:

1. How does your research move theory forward?

   _____

   _____

2. Now that you have completed your research, do you think you should have considered other theories?

   _____

   _____

Design. You should be prepared to answer the following questions about your design:

1. Were there any confounding variables in your study that you did not account for?

   _____

   _____

2. Now that your study is complete, do you still feel that this was the most appropriate design?

   _____

   _____

3. What were the problems that occurred with your design and how did you overcome them?

   _____

   _____

Literature review. Most questions about your literature review will center on any new studies that have been published since your proposal was completed.

1. How does current literature impact the conclusions and recommendations from your study?

   _____

   _____

   _____

Feasibility. You should be prepared to answer the following questions:

1. What were the major stumbling blocks that you faced in conducting your research and how did you overcome them?

   _____

   _____

   _____

2. How could your data collection time have been shortened?

   _____

   _____

   _____

3. If you had to do your study all over again, how would you do it differently?

   _____

   _____

   _____

4. What recommendations would you make to other students who are entering the dissertation phase of their research?

   _____

   _____

   _____

5. If another researcher were going to continue with your research, what recommendations would you give to him or her?

   _____

   _____

   _____

Topic: Jumping Through Hoops

Once you have successfully defended your dissertation, the first thing you need to do is pat yourself on the back. You are done with the dissertation; you have almost made it through all of the requirements for the doctoral degree and you should be congratulated. However, you have not graduated yet. There are still a number of administrative issues that need to be finished, so check with your university about the requirements you need to fulfill to complete your degree. You most likely will have final fees to pay prior to graduation. Attend to all of these as soon as possible so that you can look forward to walking across that stage at graduation without any last-minute details hanging over your head. Although all of the administrative details can be a hassle, they are certainly much easier to complete than all that you have gone through during your time as a doctoral student!

Topic: What to Make of Your Dissertation

Once you have defended the dissertation and fulfilled all of the last-minute graduation requirements—paying all of your fees and so forth—the only question left is: "what do you do with the dissertation now?" You have spent a lot of time, money and effort to get you to this point, and you have created an important product—and it's great that that product has enabled you to complete your Ph.D. and graduate, but its usefulness doesn't need to end there.

In the world of academia, your dissertation is really a part of your resume for applying for teaching positions; it will serve to let prospective employers know where your research and teaching interests lie. For some people, the dissertation is the beginning of many, many years of work in a particular area of research. They will continue to build upon the groundwork that was laid in the dissertation. This is why—way back when you were selecting your topic—it was important to choose a topic that fit in with the academic literature.

If used properly, you can get quite a bit of mileage out of the dissertation—considering the effort that went into completing it, that is a good thing. You can consider going to professional or academic conferences and presenting portions of your dissertation. While publishing the dissertation is one way of disseminating the knowledge you have created in the dissertation, many people do not read dissertations—but both professionals and academics attend conferences. By presenting your dissertation at conferences, you will be able to share the knowledge you have created.

The dissertation is a very long project. You can break the body of the dissertation up into several smaller articles. Just like presenting at conferences, this is a way of disseminating the knowledge that you created in your dissertation. This takes one publication and turns it into many, and this is very important if you plan a future in the world of academia.

You may also consider presenting workshops on your topic. This will be a consideration for dissertations that have a very practitioner-focused orientation. This might also be a way for you to make money off of your dissertation. If this avenue is available to you, it is definitely worth considering.

If you enjoy writing—and your dissertation topic is of interest to a more general audience—you may wish to turn the academic dissertation into a more popularly accessible book; as dissertations only reach a very select audience, this can be another way of sharing the knowledge you have created. This can be a particularly good consideration for qualitative dissertations—especially those that get at narratives or lived experiences.

Definition of Terms

This book uses many technical terms that are common to the dissertation process, the research process or academic writing. These are generally defined during the first instance of their use, but this section is provided as a single location resource to list many of the most important terms used throughout this book.

Action Research - a type of research that focuses on solving a problem in a workplace. This is not generally accepted approach for a dissertation.

Analysis of Variance (ANOVA) - a statistical test that looks at the difference among three or more groups. There are a variety of types of ANOVAs, including ANCOVA, MANOVA.

   Analysis of Covariance (ANCOVA) – this is actually a blend of ANOVA and regression.

   Multiple Analysis of Variance or Multivariate Analysis of Variance (MANOVA) – examines how one or more independent variables impacts the dependent variables.

   Multivariate Analysis of Covariance (MANCOVA) – an extension of ANCOVA.

Case Study - a qualitative design that looks at a bounded system (a system that has clear boundaries like a workplace or a classroom) and uses triangulation.

Causal-comparative/quasi-experimental - a quantitative design where the researcher may make some statements about causality but not as strongly as can be made with an experimental design. This design lacks the key features of a true experiment.

Chair - the dissertation Chair is the faculty member who guides your dissertation.

Chi Square – a statistical test that looks at whether observed data is different from what would result from chance; this is used for categorical data.

Code book – explains exactly what data was collected and how it was coded in a particular study.

Coding – how data is recorded in a study. For example, if the variable is gender, "female" may be coded as 1 and "male" may be coded as 0.

Committee - a group of academics who vet and guide your dissertation, assuring that it conforms to the standards of the department and university. It is comprised of a varying number of individuals (usually between three and five), who are faculty members in your own department, although they sometimes include a member from another department at your institution or even from another institution.

Comprehensive Exams (comps) - an exam that is given after the completion of coursework and prior to starting the dissertation, some schools have "qualifying exams" instead.

Concept – some qualitative researchers use this term to refer to a qualitative "variable."

Confounding variable - a variable that the researcher believes could impact the study. It is held constant so that the research is not examining it. (For example, if you are examining the impact of a specific program on delinquency prevention, gender could be a confounding variable, since girls are far less likely to be delinquent that boys. You would want to examine the data for boys and girls separately. You would also want to make sure that one of the groups in your study wasn't comprised primarily of one gender while the other group was comprised primarily of the other gender or a mix of both genders.)

Correlational Design - a quantitative design that attempts to identify the relationship between two variables.

Coursework - the classes that you will complete prior to formally starting the dissertation process.

De-identified Data – Data from which all identifiers (such as name, address, social security number) have been removed.

Descriptive Design - a quantitative design that only explains what exists in the world, it does not talk about relationships, prediction, or causation. All qualitative designs are descriptive as well.

Design – how your research is set up.

Dissertation Defense - a formal meeting that takes place between you and your committee at which you present your dissertation study after its completion; your committee members ask questions and, at the end, decide whether or not you have successfully completed the dissertation.

Ethnography - a qualitative design that looks at a culture, subculture, or microculture.

Experiment - also referred to as a "true experiment." This is a quantitative design where the researcher exercises control over the variables, there is random assignment to groups and also a control group. Statements about causality can be made when this design is used.

Grounded Theory - a qualitative design that seeks to create theory rather than test theory.

Human Subjects Research - most of our research in the social sciences involves human subjects, even if we do not directly interact with subjects and only use their artifacts for our research or utilize secondary data.

Hypothesis - this is a statement that the researcher makes about what is going on in the study. More commonly used in quantitative research as opposed to qualitative.

IRB (Institutional Review Board) - this is a panel that reviews all research at an institution for the purpose of the protection of human subjects; these panels may—depending upon the type of institution—also review other types of studies as well, such as clinical studies or animal research.

IRB Review - the review conducted by the IRB. You must receive approval for your research from your university's IRB before you can conduct any research.

    Exempt IRB Review - this is the briefest of IRB reviews and does not require the full IRB committee to review the proposal. Research that falls under this type of review is of minimal risk to subjects. It often involves secondary data and either limited or no contact with human subjects.

    Expedited IRB Review - this review is not as short as the exempt review but not nearly as lengthy as the full review. The research must be minimal risk and not involve a vulnerable population.

    Full IRB Review - this is the longest and most exacting IRB review. It requires that the full IRB committee sit and review the proposal. It may also require that special reviewers sit and review the proposal if protected populations are involved in the research.

Instrument – a tool that is used for measurement in research, such as a survey or questionnaire.

Normed, validated instrument – this is an instrument that has been tested and retested on multiple populations to insure that it measures what it purports to measure.

Longitudinal Data – data that was collected over time in a study so that the same subjects were measured more than once.

Longitudinal Study – a study that collected data during at least two time periods.

Measure – an instrument is sometimes referred to as a "measure."

Measurement – the assignment of numbers to that which the study is examining.

Meta-analysis - most institutions will not allow this type of study to be conducted for a dissertation since it is merely a comparison and summary of previous research that has been conducted—although these types of studies can be very informative when writing a literature review.

Methodology and Method - while these terms have different meanings, they are often used interchangeably. Technically, "methodology" is the study of method. "Method" refers to the particular ways in which a study is conducted. The third chapter of the dissertation is entitled either "Methodology" or "Method," but it is the chapter that provides the specific directions for how your study will be (in the case of the proposal) or was (in the case of the dissertation) carried out.

Methodological approach – within the broad methodologies of quantitative and qualitative research there are the approaches that are used to guide a study.

Narrative approach - a qualitative approach that is grounded in the story of the subject.

Phenomenology - a qualitative approach that looks at a phenomenon. These studies often seek to get at the "lived experiences" of the subjects.

Population descriptors – these are used to describe the population under study and should not be confused with "variables." In a study, a population descriptor does not vary. So, if "female" is a population descriptor, then only females are in the study population. If "gender" is a variable, both males and females must be in the study.

Primary Data - raw data that is collected by researchers for their own study. This data may be either quantitative and consist of mostly numbers or qualitative and consist mostly of words.

Proposal - this is usually the first three chapters of the dissertation and presents a framework for what you want your study to be.

Proposal Defense - this is a meeting that some schools have that takes place between you and your committee after the proposal is written to discuss the research you will be conducting.

Qualifying Exams (qualifiers) - some schools will use qualifying exams as opposed to comprehensive exams. Qualifying exams are held much earlier in your program, often at a certain point in coursework after you have taken a few basic classes. The results of these exams will determine if you remain in the program.

Qualitative Research - a research approach that generally relies upon verbal data from only a few subjects and explores those subjects in depth.

Qualitative Software Packages - these are computer packages that are used to help organize qualitative data; they do not perform analyses, but can help you analyze the data. Common software packages include NVivo, Atlas ti, and QDAP among others.

Quantitative Research - a research approach that relies upon statistics and numbers; a large number of subjects are required to be able to generalize conclusions

Quantitative Software Packages - these are computer packages that are used to perform statistics; common ones include SPSS and Excel.

Regression Analysis – a statistical procedure that examines how three or more variables are related. It is a more advanced form of a correlation.

Logistic Regression – a type of regression where the dependent variable is categorical.

Linear Regression – a type of regression where the dependent variable is continuous.

Scientific Merit – this is a determination of whether a study advances the scientific knowledge base and is solidly constructed. IRBs consider the scientific merit of a study prior to approval.

Secondary Data - Raw data that is not collected by the researcher but has either been collected by another researcher (or team of researchers) or was created in the course of some other activity, for example, information collected by an agency in the course of doing business

Sociogram - A diagram that outlines the relationships among a group of people, and is often used in ethnography.

Statistics - an analysis using numbers that is conducted to understand data. Types of common statistical approaches include chi square, regression, correlation, t-test, ANOVA. (Of course, there are many, many more and a statistical textbook should be consulted for guidance.)

t-test - a statistical test that looks at the difference between two groups.

Theory – a set of interrelated statements that scientifically explains a phenomenon.

Triangulation of Data - the collecting of multiple types of data to "get at" one particular phenomena—one of the hallmarks of the case study.

Variable – there are several types of variables in research.

Independent (experimental) variable – this is the variable that you believe has an impact on the dependent variable.

Dependent (criterion measure) variable – this is the variable that is changed by the independent variable

Control variable – this variable is believed to have an impact on the dependent variable so we hold it constant in the research

Extraneous variable – this is a variable that might impact the dependent variable but because we do not know how it works we ignore it in research.

Vulnerable population - a vulnerable population in research is a group in which there is a greater potential for harm because of characteristics of those individuals. Children are considered a vulnerable population because they lack the capacity to give informed consent. Prisoners are also a vulnerable population because they do not have the same ability as other subjects to decline participation in research. Anyone with diminished mental capacity is considered vulnerable because they may lack the understanding required to consent to research.

RESOURCES

Ethnography Resources

Agar, M. (1996) *The professional stranger: an informal introduction to ethnography*. San Diego, CA: Academic Press.

General Writing Resources

Cameron, J. (1992) *The Artist's Way. New York*: Penguin.
APA style manual – www.apastyle.org/manual/
MLA style manual – www.mlahandbook.org
Purdue owl – https://owl.english.purdue.edu/owl/

Grounded Theory Resources

Glaser, B.G. & Strauss, A.L. (1999) The *Discovery of Grounded Theory*. Mill Valley, CA : Sociology Press.
Morse, J.M., Stern, P.N., Corbin, J.M., Bowers, B., & Clarke, A.E. (2009). *Developing grounded theory: The second generation*. Walnut Creek, CA: University of Arizona Press.

Phenomenological Resources

Moustakas, C. (1994) *Phenomenological Research Methods*. Thousand Oaks, CA: Sage Publications.

Mixed Methods Resources

Tashakori, A. & Teddlie, C. (2003) *Handbook of mixed methods in the social and behavioral research*. Thousand Oaks, CA: Sage Publications.

Case Study Resources

Stake, R.E. (1995) The *Art of Case Study Research*. Thousand Oaks, CA: Sage Publications.

Theory Resources

www.changingminds.org

Statistics References

Blalock, Hubert M. (1979) *Social Statistics*. McGraw-Hill

Secondary Data References

Inter-university Consortium for Political and Social Research – www.icpsr.umich.edu
Center for Medicare and Medicaid Services –cms.hhs.gov/researchers/
U.S. Census Bureau –www.census.gove/main/www/access.html
National Data Archive on Child Abuse and Neglect – www.ndacan.cornell.edu
Centers for Disease Control and Prevention –
    www.cdc.gov/nchs/nhanes/nhanes_questionnaires.htm

52469760R00064

Made in the USA
Lexington, KY
30 May 2016